First World War
and Army of Occupation
War Diary
France, Belgium and Germany

59 DIVISION
177 Infantry Brigade
Leicestershire Regiment
2/4th Battalion
24 February 1917 - 31 May 1918

WO95/3022/4

The Naval & Military Press Ltd
www.nmarchive.com
Published in association with The National Archives

Published by

The Naval & Military Press Ltd

Unit 10 Ridgewood Industrial Park,

Uckfield, East Sussex,

TN22 5QE England

Tel: +44 (0) 1825 749494

www.naval-military-press.com

www.nmarchive.com

This diary has been reprinted in facsimile from the original. Any imperfections are inevitably reproduced and the quality may fall short of modern type and cartographic standards.

© Crown Copyright
Images reproduced by permission of The National Archives, London, England, 2015.

Contents

Document type	Place/Title	Date From	Date To
Heading	WO95/3022-4 1917 Feb-1918 May 2/4 Battalion Leicestershire Regiment		
Heading	59th Division 177th Infy Bde 2-4th Bn Leicesters. Feb 1917-May 1918		
War Diary	Fovant	24/02/1917	24/02/1917
War Diary	Havre	25/02/1917	25/02/1917
War Diary	Pontdumetz	26/02/1917	28/02/1917
War Diary	Bay On Villiers	01/03/1917	06/03/1917
War Diary	Foucaucourt	07/03/1917	08/03/1917
War Diary	Belloy	09/03/1917	11/03/1917
War Diary	P.C.Marcheau	11/03/1917	16/03/1917
War Diary	P.C.Martin	17/03/1917	21/03/1917
War Diary	Foucaucourt	21/03/1917	21/03/1917
War Diary	Eterpigny	26/03/1917	26/03/1917
War Diary	Le Mesnil	27/03/1917	27/03/1917
War Diary	Cartigny	30/03/1917	31/03/1917
Operation(al) Order(s)	2/4th Leicestershire Regt: Order No. 6.		
Operation(al) Order(s)	2/4th Leicestershire Regiment Operation Order no 7	17/03/1917	17/03/1917
War Diary	Cartigny	01/04/1917	01/04/1917
War Diary	Hervilly	02/04/1917	04/04/1917
War Diary	Roisel	09/04/1917	09/04/1917
War Diary	In The Field	11/04/1917	14/04/1917
Miscellaneous	2/4th Leicestershire Regt.	19/03/1917	19/03/1917
Miscellaneous	2/4th Leicestershire Regt	18/03/1917	18/03/1917
War Diary	In The Field	16/04/1917	19/04/1917
War Diary	Bernes	28/04/1917	28/04/1917
War Diary	Cartigny	01/04/1917	01/04/1917
War Diary	Hervilly	02/04/1917	04/04/1917
War Diary	Roisel	09/04/1917	09/04/1917
War Diary	In The Field	11/04/1917	19/04/1917
War Diary	Bernes	28/04/1917	28/04/1917
War Diary	L,22 C.60.62 C NE	01/05/1917	02/05/1917
War Diary	Le Verguier 62 B N.W.	04/05/1917	07/05/1917
War Diary	Le Verguier	07/05/1917	11/05/1917
War Diary	Le Verguier 62c NE	11/05/1917	15/05/1917
War Diary	Bias Wood	20/05/1917	22/05/1917
War Diary	Equancourt 57c SE	25/05/1917	28/05/1917
War Diary	Sheet. 57c	31/05/1917	31/05/1917
War Diary	Dessart Wood 57c S.E. W.i.a.94	01/06/1917	04/06/1917
War Diary	57c Se.r.7.29 To Q 12.6.80	06/06/1917	06/06/1917
War Diary	Q.18.6.9.8	08/06/1917	14/06/1917
War Diary	Gouzeaucourt Wood Q.28.a.19.	17/06/1917	20/06/1917
War Diary	Equancourt V.16.a.61.	21/06/1917	29/06/1917
War Diary	Q 10d.3.7. Ref.map 57 C.S.E	01/07/1917	01/07/1917
War Diary	Equancourt	01/07/1917	01/07/1917
War Diary	Q 10.d.3.7 Ref.map 57 C.S.E	02/07/1917	05/07/1917
War Diary	Metz	05/07/1917	10/07/1917
War Diary	Barastre	11/07/1917	28/07/1917
War Diary	Barastre 57c O.16.d Central	01/08/1917	14/08/1917
War Diary	Barastre	15/08/1917	22/08/1917

Type	Location	Start	End
War Diary	Senlis (Sheet 57 D.p.10.d.0.4.	23/08/1917	31/08/1917
War Diary	Winnezeele J.4.d.6.5	01/09/1917	20/09/1917
War Diary	D.20.a.8.5 (Ref Gravenstafel Map Attached)	24/09/1917	25/09/1917
War Diary	D.20.a.8.5	28/09/1917	30/09/1917
Miscellaneous	2/4th Leicestershire Regiment	24/09/1917	24/09/1917
Miscellaneous	Detailed Account Of Operations	30/09/1917	30/09/1917
War Diary	Vlamertinghe	01/10/1917	02/10/1917
War Diary	Thiennes	06/10/1917	06/10/1917
War Diary	Beaumetz	08/10/1917	08/10/1917
War Diary	Thiennes	04/10/1917	04/10/1917
War Diary	Beaumetz	09/10/1917	10/10/1917
War Diary	Dieval	11/10/1917	11/10/1917
War Diary	Houdain	12/10/1917	12/10/1917
War Diary	Gouy Servins	13/10/1917	13/10/1917
War Diary	Lens Canal 56 Central	14/10/1917	17/10/1917
War Diary	Lens Canal T 3 A 4.2.	18/10/1917	22/10/1917
War Diary	Gouy Servins	23/10/1917	29/10/1917
War Diary	Lievin M27 650.30	30/10/1917	31/10/1917
Miscellaneous	Patrol Report		
War Diary	Lievin M.27 6 4 5	01/11/1917	06/11/1917
War Diary	M30a 48	07/11/1917	14/11/1917
War Diary	Souchez 58 A Central Chateau De La Haie	15/11/1917	17/11/1917
War Diary	Hauteville J35c 8.8	18/11/1917	19/11/1917
War Diary	Bailleulval 4h.65.65	20/11/1917	21/11/1917
War Diary	Achiet-Le-Petit 5I 8.5	22/11/1917	23/11/1917
War Diary	Dessart Wood Q1d 3.8.	24/11/1917	27/11/1917
War Diary	Flesquires K 18 C 7.4	28/11/1917	28/11/1917
War Diary	Lajustice L2c81	29/11/1917	30/11/1917
Miscellaneous	Patrol Report	10/11/1917	10/11/1917
Miscellaneous	Patrol Report	11/11/1917	11/11/1917
War Diary	La Justice L2c81.57c	01/12/1917	01/12/1917
War Diary	Bourlon Wood F13c82	02/12/1917	02/12/1917
War Diary	F13 D 67	03/12/1917	03/12/1917
War Diary	F13 C 82	04/12/1917	04/12/1917
War Diary	K35 B45.40	05/12/1917	10/12/1917
War Diary	Q4 D 3.2	11/12/1917	14/12/1917
War Diary	Lechelle P 25 B.45.50	15/12/1917	16/12/1917
War Diary	P 7c8.8	17/12/1917	17/12/1917
War Diary	Q 4d 32	18/12/1917	18/12/1917
War Diary	K24 637.	19/12/1917	22/12/1917
War Diary	K 35a2525	23/12/1917	23/12/1917
War Diary	Rocquigny O27d6.7.	24/12/1917	24/12/1917
War Diary	O27d6.7.	25/12/1917	25/12/1917
War Diary	Ligneruil 121b 33 Sheet 51C	26/12/1917	31/01/1918
Miscellaneous	Headquarters 177th Inf Bde	01/03/1918	01/03/1918
War Diary	Ligneruil 51c.121.b.3.3.	01/02/1918	10/02/1918
War Diary	Bavincourt 51c P 34 D.8.6	10/02/1918	10/02/1918
War Diary	Blaireville 57.c.x.4d 3.2	11/02/1918	11/02/1918
War Diary	Armagh Camp 51.b 523 C 4.4.	12/02/1918	12/02/1918
War Diary	U.28.c.8.4	13/02/1918	18/02/1918
War Diary	Mory 57.c.b22.a.7.3	19/02/1918	22/02/1918
War Diary	Mory	23/02/1918	24/02/1918
War Diary	Bullecourt	24/02/1918	28/02/1918
Operation(al) Order(s)	2/4th Leicestershire Regiment Order No 66	08/02/1918	08/02/1918
Operation(al) Order(s)	2/4th Leicestershire Regiment Order No. 67	09/02/1918	09/02/1918
Operation(al) Order(s)	2/4th Leicestershire Regiment Order No. 68	10/08/1916	10/08/1916

Type	Description	Date From	Date To
Operation(al) Order(s)	2/4th Leicestershire Regiment Order No. 69	10/08/1918	10/08/1918
Operation(al) Order(s)	2/4th Leicestershire Regiment. Order No. 71		
Map	Gravenstafel		
Heading	59th Division. 177th Infantry Brigade War Diary 2/4th Battalion The Leicestershire Regiment March 1918		
War Diary	Bullecourt	01/03/1918	19/03/1918
War Diary	Mory	20/03/1918	23/03/1918
War Diary	Ervillers	23/03/1918	25/03/1918
War Diary	D-Les-Ayettes	26/03/1918	26/03/1918
War Diary	Bienvillers	27/03/1918	27/03/1918
War Diary	Sus-St-Leger	28/03/1918	29/03/1918
War Diary	Houdain	30/03/1918	30/03/1918
War Diary	Beugin	31/03/1918	31/03/1918
War Diary		21/03/1918	25/03/1918
Heading	177th Brigade. 59th Division. 2/4th Battalion Leicestershire Regiment April 1918 /May 1918		
War Diary	Beugin.	01/04/1918	01/04/1918
War Diary	L.3.6. Sheet.27.	02/04/1918	04/04/1918
War Diary	St Jean Camp I 3.6.3.4	05/04/1918	10/04/1918
War Diary	Zonnebeke D21.d.9.2	11/04/1918	12/04/1918
War Diary	St Lawrence Camp Brandhoek	13/04/1918	13/04/1918
War Diary	Berthem.	14/04/1918	14/04/1918
War Diary	S 5a Sheet 28	15/04/1918	16/04/1918
War Diary	Southill Camp M.17.d.0.0	17/04/1918	17/04/1918
War Diary	Windmill Camp	18/04/1918	18/04/1918
War Diary	M29.a.4.8	19/04/1918	19/04/1918
War Diary	Reninghelst	20/04/1918	20/04/1918
War Diary	Dirty Bucket Camp Vlamertinghe	21/04/1918	21/04/1918
War Diary	E.7.c.3.1	22/04/1918	26/04/1918
War Diary	School Camp Watou	27/04/1918	27/04/1918
War Diary	G25.d.6.9	28/04/1918	30/04/1918
Miscellaneous	2/4th Bn Leicestershire Regt.	14/04/1918	14/04/1918
War Diary	G25d6.9	01/05/1918	05/05/1918
War Diary	Sheet 27 E20 HQ.6	06/05/1918	06/05/1918
War Diary	Nieurlet-A	07/05/1918	09/05/1918
War Diary	Mametz	10/05/1918	10/05/1918
War Diary	Pressy-Les Pernes	11/05/1918	14/05/1918
War Diary	Estree-Cauchie	15/05/1918	31/05/1918

WO/95/3022/4

1919 Feb - 1916 My
2/4 Battalion Lancashire
Regiment.

59TH DIVISION
177TH INFY BDE

2-4TH BN LEICESTERS.
FEB 1917 - MAY 1918.

AND (ABSORBED BY 14 BN)

1916 JAN & FEB

TO UK JUNE 1918

SECRET

177/59

WAR DIARY 2/4 Leicestershire Regt

Army Form C. 2118.

INTELLIGENCE SUMMARY.
(Erase heading not required.)

February 1917

Instructions regarding War Diaries and Intelligence Summaries are contained in F. S. Regs., Part II. and the Staff Manual respectively. Title pages will be prepared in manuscript.

Hour, Date, Place	Summary of Events and Information	Remarks and references to Appendices
FOVANT 24/2/17	Battn left FOVANT CAMP for SOUTHAMPTON	177/59 C.I.
HAVRE 25/2/17	Battn arrived HAVRE 2:30 A.M. & proceeded to Rest Camp at 5.30 A.M.	
HAVRE 25/2/17	Left HAVRE 9.20 p.m. for PONT du METZ	
PONT du METZ 26/2/17	arrived PONT du METZ 4 p.m.	
" 27/2/17	B" rested at Pont du METZ	
28/2/17	B" left PONT du METZ for FOUENCAMPS arriving 4 p.m.	

H.F. Mellis Lt.Col.
cmdg 2/4 Leicester Regt

9/3/17

2/4th Leicester

SECRET Army Form C. 2118.

MARCH 1917

WAR DIARY
or
INTELLIGENCE SUMMARY

(Erase heading not required.)

Place	Hour, Date	Summary of Events and Information	Remarks and references to Appendices
BAYONVILLIERS	1.3.17	Bn. moved from FOUCAUCAMP to Cr. 59 Camp BAYONVILLIERS	F.D.
BAYONVILLIERS	2.3.17 to 6.3.17	Resting at Cr. 59 Camp.	F.D.
FOUCAUCOURT	7.3.17	Bn moved to FOUCAUCOURT arriving 3.10 pm	F.D.
"	8.3.17	Bn. left FOUCAUCOURT at 6.45 pm for BELLOY occupied reserve trenches. P.C. RUDOLPHE 11 a.m.	F.D.
BELLOY	9.3.17 to 11.3.17	Remained in support at BELLOY. 4 men killed in morning 9/11th through German shell striking up dugout. Bn. moved up to front line. 11 go at P.C. MARCHEAU.	F.D.
P.C. MARCHEAU	11.3.17		F.D.
"	13.3.17	2/Lt H.W. HUTCHINSON killed by sniper at T.4 a.5.4	

(73989) W4141—463. 400,000. 9/14. H.&J.Ltd. Forms/C. 2118/10.

SECRET

b/n Lincoln Regt
MARCH 1917

Army Form C. 2118.

WAR DIARY
or
INTELLIGENCE SUMMARY.
(Erase heading not required.)

Instructions regarding War Diaries and Intelligence Summaries are contained in F.S. Regs., Part II. and the Staff Manual respectively. Title pages will be prepared in manuscript.

Hour, Date, Place	Summary of Events and Information	Remarks and references to Appendices
P.C. MARCHEAU. 16.3.17.	Special Orders received with regard to movement of Troops in front. Our operation orders attached	J.S.
P.C. MARTIN 17.3.17	Germans having wheeled B" ind forced to occupy German trenches, Hqrs at T.4.d.6.4. Our operation orders attached.	J.S.
" 16.3.17	Standing Patrols sent out to	J.S.
" 18.3.17 to 21.3.17	Patrol Intelligence + Reconnaissance Reports ab to movements of enemy attached	J.S.
FOUCAUCOURT. 21.3.17	B" returned to rest at FOUCAUCOURT arriving 4:30pm.	J.S.

2/4 Leicester Regt

SECRET

Army Form C. 2118.

WAR DIARY
or
INTELLIGENCE SUMMARY.
(Erase heading not required.)

MARCH

Hour, Date, Place	Summary of Events and Information	Remarks and references to Appendices
ETERPIGNY 26.3.17	Battalion moved from FOUCAUCOURT to ETERPIGNY	
Gd MESNIL 27.3.17	Battalion moved from ETERPIGNY to Gd MESNIL and remained in front until 30th	
CARTIGNY 30.3.17	Battalion moved to CARTIGNY	
" 31.3.17	Battalion moved to HAMELET in support to 5th LEICESTERS during attack on AESBECOURT and HERVILLY returning to CARTIGNY with one Company; three Companies being attached to 5th Leicesters as covering parties	

(73989) W4141—463. 400,000. 9/14. H.&J.Ltd. Forms/C. 2118/10.

2/4th Leicestershire Regt: Order No.6.

Copy No.

1. In order to assist operations of troops to the south of us on March 17th/18th the 59th Division will be prepared to simulate an attack by wire cutting, night firing, general bombardment and discharge of smoke.

2. From Zero hour to Zero hour plus 5 minutes the 50th Divisional Artillery will cover the front line from APES-WOOD inclusive to the ESTREES-VILLERS CARBONNEL ROAD with barrage fire.

3. One 177th Light T.M. Battery will take part in above bombardment.

4. The 177th Machine Gun Company will assist the barrage.

5. From Zero hour until Zero hour plus 5 minutes the Battalion will discharge smoke along the whole front if the wind is favourable.
The following code will be used to notify Companies as to wind.
    LONDON   wind favourable.
    PARIS   wind unfavourable.
Smoke candles will be distributed to give one candle to every four yards of frontage.

6. O.C. Companies will arrange for continuous night firing from rifles and Lewis guns with the object of keeping open the guns cut in the enemy wire.

7. Zero hour will be notified later.

8. 2 runners per Company will report at B.H.Q. with watches at 3.0 pm 17th inst: for the purpose of syncronizing watches.

9. In view of the certainty of retaliation all men not required for lighting candles or essential for the immediate safety of the line, must be in dug-outs and places of safety.

10. Patrols will not be sent out.

11. Rations and water have been supplied tonight for 48 hours.

12. Acknowledge by wire or runner.

Copy No. 1   Filed.
"   "   2   177th Bde: Hdqrs:
"   "   3   A Coy:
"   "   4   B "
"   "   5   C "
"   "   6   D "
"   "   7   Hqrd Coy:

F. Stevenson
Capt: & Adjt:
2/4th Leicestershire Regiment.

2/4th LEICESTERSHIRE REGIMENT.   Copy No.....
==================================   Operation order No 7

Ref. Sheet 62c S.W.   17/3/17.

1. A & B Coys: will push out strong patrols with
   Lewis guns to occupy the line CROCODILE TRENCH-
   ANNIBAL TRENCH.
   B Coy: from T11. 6. 0. 9 to T5 d 7.6
   A Coy: from T5-d 7.6 to T6 a.1.5.
   B Coy: will gain touch with 2/6th S.Staffords
   Regt: on right.
   A Coy: will gain touch with 2/5th Leicester
   Regt: on the left.
   The remainder of these two companies will occupy
   suitable support trenches in rear, which will be
   consolidated.

   D Coy: will occupy and consolidate CHERIF TRENCH.
   C Coy: will occupy the dugouts in old line at
   present held by B Coy:

2. Sappers will be attached to each company in order
   to discover mines.

3. Reports as to new Coy: Hdqrs: to be sent in, and
   rations and water will be sent up.

4. Dump for tools, S.A.A. etc. is at T4.6.1.5½

5. R.A.P. at P.C. MARCEAU.

6. Patrols are forbidden to take any letters or
   papers liable to disclose the identity of the
   Brigade or Division.

7. Reports to B Coy: old Hdqrs:

8. Acknowledge.

Copy No.1 Filed.
  "   " 2 177th Brigade.
  "   " 3 A Coy:
  "   " 4 B "
  "   " 5 C "
  "   " 6 D "

17/3/17.   (sd)H.F.Wallis, LtCol:
                                  Cmmdg: C/S.

59

WAR DIARY
~~INTELLIGENCE SUMMARY~~
(Erase heading not required.)

4th Newcastle Regt
Vol 3
April 1917

Army Form C. 2118.

Hour, Date, Place	Summary of Events and Information	Remarks and references to Appendices
11-30 A.M. 1/4/17 CARTIGNY	The Battalion moved to HERVILLY	AM3
8-0 P.M. 2/4/17 HERVILLY	The Battalion attacked FERVAQUE FARM. 2 Companys in front line, 1 Company in support and 1 Company in reserve. On approaching the objective it was found to be heavily wired and impossible to get through. Repeated attempts were made to cut through the wire. Heavy machine gunfire was opened from the flanks by the enemy and at 3.30 A.M. 3/4/17 the order was given to withdraw.	AM3
11-30 P.M. 4/4/17 HERVILLY.	The Battalion moved to ROISEL to rest. Reliefs being relieved by 2/5 NORTH STAFFS.	AM3
8-0 P.M. 9/4/17 ROISEL.	The Battalion relieved 2/4th Lincoln Regt in the line from MARGICOURT to FERVAQUE FARM. "B" and "D" Companys in front line.	AM3
4-0 P.M. 11/4/17 IN THE FIELD	The Battalion frontage was extended from FERVAQUE FARM to GRAND PRIEL WOODS SOUTH. "C" Company taking over new frontage.	AM3
9-30 P.M. 13/4/17 IN THE FIELD	Patrol was sent out to the CHATEAU East of GRAND PRIEL WOODS SOUTH. This was found to be unoccupied and was immediately occupied by patrol.	AM3
8-30 P.M. 14/4/17 IN THE FIELD	Two posts were pushed forward 700 yards between KAFFIR COPSE and GRAND PRIEL WOODS NORTH and occupied.	AM3
9-0 P.M. 14/4/17 IN THE FIELD	A patrol was sent out to occupy cottage east of GRAND PRIEL WOODS NORTH and rifle pits NE of cottage. After a short but sharp encounter with the enemy the cottage was occupied. Cpl M.Fewitt being conspicuous for his coolness. The rifle pits were found to be thoroughly trenched to enfilade fire, the pits were impossible to hold so the patrol was withdrawn to the cottage.	AM3

Tom Stephenson Lt. Col.

2/4th Leicestershire Regt.

Patrol report. March 19th/17.

A patrol left our lines at 10.0am this morning consisting of 1 18th Hlept, and 6 men. The patrol crossed the canal and river SOMME by the WEST SUBURB-ST CHRIST temporary foot bridge. It patrolled to the EAST of the river SOMME as far as Cemetery N.E. of ENNEMAIN V.18.B.2.4. Nothing was seen of the enemy but a patrol of Lovat's scouts informed the patrol that they had seen a mounted enemy patrol at V.18.C.7.0.
The patrol returned at 4.30 pm

2/4th Leicestershire Regt.

Patrol report.   March 18/17

"A patrol went out from T5.6.1.0 as far as BRIOST. From there it turned to the right and patrolled the bank of the SOMME as far as U.8.b.6.3 where the bridge across the river has been destroyed. No signs of enemy were seen. The patrol returned at 1.0 am 19/3/17 having been out five hours."

WAR DIARY or INTELLIGENCE SUMMARY

Army Form C. 2118.

2/4th Leicestershire Regt.

April 1917

(Erase heading not required.)

Hour, Date, Place	Summary of Events and Information	Remarks and references to Appendices
9.30 P.M. 16/4/17 IN THE FIELD	A post was pushed forward 500 yards in front of CHATEAU between Cottage and GRAND PRIEL FARM and occupied.	P.M.B.
10.30 P.M. 19/4/17 IN THE FIELD	The Battalion was relieved by 2/8th Sherwood Foresters and moved to BERNES to rest billets.	P.M.B.
12.30 P.M. 28/4/17 BERNES.	The Battalion relieved 2/6th NORTH STAFFS in support line from LE VERGUIER to NORTH of PIEUMEL WOODS.	P.M.B.

Tini Clayton Lt Col

WAR DIARY *1st Leicestershire Regt*

Army Form C. 2118.

or

INTELLIGENCE SUMMARY

(Erase heading not required.)

April 1917

Hour, Date, Place	Summary of Events and Information	Remarks and references to Appendices
11·30 A.M. 1/4/17 CARTIGNY	The Battalion moved to HERVILLY	AM3
8·0 P.M. 2/4/17 HERVILLY	The Battalion attacked FERVAQUE FARM. 2 Company's in front line, 1 Company in support and 1 Company in reserve. In approaching the objective it was found to be heavily wired and unsuccessfully to get through. Repeated attempts were made to cut through the wire. Heavy machine gun fire was opened from the flanks by the enemy and at 3·30 am 3/4/17 the order was given to withdraw.	AM3
11·30 P.M. 4/4/17 HERVILLY	The Battalion moved to ROISEL to rest Battns being relieved by 2/5th NORTH STAFFS.	AM3
8·0 P.M. 9/4/17 ROISEL	The Battalion relieved 1st Lincoln Regt in the line from MARICOURT to FERVAQUE FARM. "B" and "D" Companys in front line.	AM3
4·0 P.M. 11/4/17 IN THE FIELD	The Battalion frontage was extended from FERVAQUE FARM to GRAND PRIEL WOODS South. "C" Company taking over new frontage.	AM3
9·30 P.M. 13/4/17 IN THE FIELD	Patrol was sent out to the CHATEAU 600 ft GRAND PRIEL WOODS South. This was found to be unoccupied and was immediately occupied by patrol.	AM3
8·30 P.M. 14/4/17 IN THE FIELD	Two 6 ft ST Vickers pushed forward 700 yards between KAFFIR COPSE and GRAND PRIEL WOODS NORTH and occupied.	AM3
9·0 P.M. 14/4/17 IN THE FIELD	A patrol was sent out to occupy cottage east of GRAND PRIEL WOODS North and Rifle Pits NE of cottage. After a short but sharp encounter with the enemy the cottage was occupied. Cpl N. Fleurett being conspicuous for his coolness of skill This was found to be unoccupied and trying to enfilade fire on this loose improve the kholl so the patrol was with drawn to the cottage	AM3

Signed Graham Lt Col

WAR DIARY
or
INTELLIGENCE SUMMARY.
(Erase heading not required.)

7th Leicestershire Regt.   Army Form C. 2118.

April 1917.

Hour, Date, Place	Summary of Events and Information	Remarks and references to Appendices
9.30 P.M. 16/4/17 IN THE FIELD	A post was pushed forward 500 yards in front of CHATEAU between RANGE and GRAND PRIEL FARM and occupied.	PKB
10.30 P.M. 19/4/17 IN THE FIELD	The Battalion was relieved by 2/8th Sherwood Foresters and moved to BERNES to RESt BRIEF.	PKB
1.30 P.M. 28/4/17 BERNES.	The Battalion relieved 1/6 North Staffs in Support line from LE VERGUIER to NORTH of PIEUMEL WOODS.	PKB.

Tim Clephane Lt Col
1 min Clephane Lt Col

SECRET ORIGINAL

177/59

WAR DIARY
or
INTELLIGENCE SUMMARY
(Erase heading not required.)

2/4 Leicestershire Regt.   Army Form C. 2118.

MAY 1917

177/59

Hour, Date, Place	Summary of Events and Information	Remarks and references to Appendices
1-5-17	2/Lieut P. William proceeded to England on leave.	
9-30 PM 2-5-17 L.22.c.60. 62C NE	The Battalion relieved 2/5 Leicestershire Regt in the Front Line from Ascension Farm to 2000 yards N.N.E. of Farm L.18.c.72. Battalion Headquarters did not move.	9MB
10 PM 4-5-17 Le Verguier 62 B N.W.	An Officer Patrol was sent out from our forward Post G.19.d.29. on the direction of Buisson-Gaulaine Farm and was fired on by enemy patrol. Our patrol opened fire on enemy then returned. 300 yards. Patrol then returned.	9MB
6-5-17	2/Lieut H.N. Taylor reported for duty.	9MB
7-5-17	Hexicourt on a course. Capt. E. Brown proceeded to relief N.S. White Brevet Armand of C Company.	9MB
9.30 PM 7-5-17, Le Verguier	2/Lieut T.P. Southby wounded. The Battalion was relieved by 2/5 Leicestershire Regt and took over the Support Line North of Le Verguier to 150 yards South of Brosse Woods. L.21.d.55.	9MB
11-5-17	2/Lieut A.N.J. Watts reported for duty.	9MB
9-30 PM 11-5-17 Le Verguier 62C NE	The Battalion relieved 2/5 Leicestershire Regt in the Front Line from Ascension Farm to 2000 yards N.N.E. of Farm L.18.c.72.	9MB
10-30 PM 15-5-17. Le Verguier 62C S.E.	The Battalion was relieved by the Poona Horse and proceeded to hut camp at Bias Wood. T.15.c.03.	9MB
20-5-17 Bias Wood	2/Lieut P. Waldren returned from leave. Brigade Church Parade. Cards of distinguished Service in the field were presented to Sergt W. Wright & Company and Pte F. Stevens C. Company	9MB

Reorganising.   M. Jones Major
Commanding 2/4 Leicestershire Regt.

Army Form C. 2118.

WAR DIARY
2/4TH LEICESTERSHIRE REGT
or
INTELLIGENCE SUMMARY.
(Erase heading not required.)

MAY 1917

Instructions regarding War Diaries and Intelligence Summaries are contained in F.S. Regs., Part II. and the Staff Manual respectively. Title pages will be prepared in manuscript.

Hour, Date, Place	Summary of Events and Information	Remarks and references to Appendices
21-5-17 BUS WOOD	2/Lieut: W.R. SOUTER admitted to Hospital	9K13.
22-5-17 BUS WOOD	Lieut R.ST J. SHARP reported for duty	9K13.
6.A.M. 25-5-17 EQUANCOURT 57°SE	The Battalion moved to EQUANCOURT by march route and encamped at V.16.c.7.3.	9K13.
2.PM. 28-5-17 EQUANCOURT 57°SE.	The Battalion moved into Camp at V.11.c.77. 2nd Lt E.A. SHAUL took over duties of Town Major of EQUANCOURT.	9K13.
3.P.M. 31-5-17 SHEET. 57c	The Battalion moved into Camp at DESSART WOOD W1.B.17. MAJOR J.C. BAINES proceeded to CALAIS suffering from Nerves MAJOR R.A. HENDERSON assumed duty as 2nd in command.	9K13.

Raperdus V. MAJOR
Commanding 2/4 Leicestershire Regt.

SECRET ORIGINAL

59/1/17

Army Form C. 2118.

2/4th LEICESTERSHIRE REGT

WAR DIARY
~~INTELLIGENCE SUMMARY~~

(Erase heading not required.)

JUNE 1917

177/59

Instructions regarding War Diaries and Intelligence Summaries are contained in F.S. Regs., Part II. and the Staff Manual respectively. Title pages will be prepared in manuscript.

Hour, Date, Place	Summary of Events and Information	Remarks and references to Appendices
1-6-17 DESSART WOOD 57c S.E. W.I.a.94.	Lt Col. SIR IAN COLQUHOUN. BART. D.S.O. admitted to Hospital. MAJOR R.A. HENDERSON. Assumes Command of the Battalion. CAPT. A. SILVER assumes 2nd in Command 2nd/LIEUT. M. HAINES assumes Command of A. Coy. 2nd LIEUT. V.C. LOWRY AND 2nd/LIEUT T.C. SMITH proceeded to FOUCAUCOURT For Lewis Gun and Trench Mortar course.	A.B.
2-6-17 DESSART WOOD W.I.a.94.	2nd/LIEUT H.E. CATLOW admitted to Hospital Reinforcement draft of 10 O.R.	A.B.
3-6-17. DESSART WOOD W.I.a.94.	Battalion Church Parade. SERGT H. FEWITT presented with the CROIX-DE-GUERRE. For distinguished bravery in the field on the night 8 14/15 APRIL 1917.	A.B.
4-6-17. DESSART WOOD W.I.a.94.	2nd LIEUT. H.E. CATLOW Invalided to ENGLAND	A.B.
6-6-17 57c S.E. R.7.d.29.6. Q.2.Z.80.	The Battalion relieved the 2/6TH LEICESTERSHIRE REGT in the Front line NORTH OF VILLIERS - PLOUICH. Two Companies in Front line. One in Support, One in Reserve. 2nd/LIEUT W.R. SOWTER. Returned to Duty from Hospital 2nd/LIEUT. A.A. CLARKE admitted to Hospital.	A.B.

Major
Comm. 2/4 Leicestershire Regt.

WAR DIARY
or
INTELLIGENCE SUMMARY

(Erase heading not required.)

Army Form C. 2118.

1/4TH LEICESTERSHIRE REGT.

JUNE 1917

Hour, Date, Place	Summary of Events and Information	Remarks and references to Appendices
8-6-17. Q.18.E.9.8.	Our Artillery bombarded the German Trenches from 9.0 p.m. to 9.51 p.m. and 11-8 p.m. to 11-5 p.m.	
9-6-17. Q.18.E.98.	Our Artillery bombarded the German Trenches from 9.30 p.m. to 9.40 p.m. Reinforcement draft of 4 O.R. from CALAIS.	
11-6-17. Q.18.E.98.	B and D Coys. relieve A and C Coys. in the Front line. A Coy. in Support. C. Coy. in Reserve. A fighting Patrol of 2 Officers. (Capt: A. SILVER AND LIEUT: L.B. ORCHARD) 35. O.R's. with two Lewis Guns went out from our Advance Post at R.7.8.17. with the Objects (a) To examine German wire in R.I.d. and R.7.8. (b) To capture prisoners from German Patrols or Working Parties. Some old German wire was reached at R.7.8.18. which delayed progress for some time. Patrol then proceeded towards R.7.3.69. The wire was examined and found to be a long trap variety, thickly interlaced with strong barbed wire. This continued for some distance to R.7.8. 10.80. and in the opposite direction to R.I.d.14. where there was a gap covered by a German Machine Gun. To enemy Patrols were met. But a party of Snipers got to the flank and worried the Patrol considerably. Several German's were seen passing up and down the wire and repairing it in places. A Lewis Gun party was heard digging at R.I.d.14. The Patrol returned at 1-45 a.m.	Signed J.B. Jones Lieut Colonel Commdg 1/4 Leicestershire Regt

Army Form C. 2118.

WAR DIARY
or
INTELLIGENCE SUMMARY

(Erase heading not required.)

2/4 7TH LEICESTERSHIRE REG.T

JUNE 1917

Hour, Date, Place	Summary of Events and Information	Remarks and references to Appendices
12-6-17. Q.18.B.98.	A patrol of 1 Officer (Lieut. L.B. Orchard) 6 O.R. went out from our Advance Post at R.7.B.17 to intercept enemy patrols between them and the German wire. A position at about R.7.B.19 was taken up with the left flank on the VILLIERS- PLOUICH - RIBECOURT Road. Nothing was seen until about 1 a.m. when a large patrol was observed coming towards our lines. The patrol withdrew towards wire of pole post (R.7.B.17). Enemy patrol advanced a little further and apparently waited to reconnoitre their position. Our patrol fired on their strength no lights were used but a very light outs fired from their wire and their direction, After 2 few moments the enemy patrol which to their wire and opened 50 yards, the enemy patrol which to their wire and opened up a heavy fire which S.A. their Machine Guns joined in. Our patrol withdrew at 1.45 a.m. Reinforcement draft of 1 NCO 4 O.R arrived.	O.R.10.
13-6-17. Q.18.B.98.	A patrol of 2 Officers (Capt A. Silver and Lieut. L.B. Orchard) 12 O.R. went out from the advance post at R.7.B.17 to locate enemy patrols. The wire was cut to the right of (N°2. post. (R.7.B.17.) and a team of 60 may was marched on. No enemy patrols were put in White Side of Enemy wire. The enemy Verey was reached at R.7.B.79. Immediately a searchlight about 50 yds's to our left & 50 yds's behind Trenton wire started to search from a point in front of wire. A Machine Gun looking in conjunction with the Searchlight started traversing their wire but stopped at 3 yds.	Commdg 2/4 Leicestershire Regt.

Army Form C. 2118.

WAR DIARY

2/4TH LEICESTERSHIRE REGT

INTELLIGENCE SUMMARY

JUNE 1917.

(Erase heading not required.)

Instructions regarding War Diaries and Intelligence Summaries are contained in F.S. Regs., Part II. and the Staff Manual respectively. Title pages will be prepared in manuscript.

Hour, Date, Place	Summary of Events and Information	Remarks and references to Appendices
13-6-17.	From our Lgt. Hank, Serjt Berry and Pte Papworth shared great coolness in cutting a gap J.H. wide in the German wire which was 15 feet thick (Baker then started to go through the gap to capture German Machine Gun when on the Ricy of Body of 40 Germans suddenly appeared at Machine Gun Post. Our patrol then withdrew (at 2am) Capt. F. Dickinson returned to duty from hospital. Reinforcement draft of 3 OT's arrive. Concentrated bombardment of III Corps Artillery on Ribécourt. (L.25 Central of line)	AKB.
14-6-17. Q.18.J.98.	Our Artillery bombarded the German trenches at 11:30 p.m. 2nd Lieut E.G. Talley returned to duty from Foucaucourt.	AKB.
17-6-17. GOUZEAUCOURT WOOD Q.28.a.19.	The Battalion was relieved by 2/5 7th LEICESTERSHIRE REGT and went into Support at Gouzeaucourt Wood. Q28.a.19. AKB. Capt. E. Browne returned to duty from FLEXICOURT.	AKB.
18-6-17. GOUZEAUCOURT WOOD Q.28.a.19.	Capt. E. Browne admitted to hospital.	AKB.
20-6-17.	Capt. E.G. Smith, Lieut R.J. Sharp, 2nd Lieut A.W. Watts, 2nd Lieut T.C. Smith, 2nd Lieut V.C. Lowry, 2nd Lieut H. Cross and 120 OR proceed to Pont-Remy on Musketry course.	AKB.
21-6-17. EQUANCOURT V.16.a.61.	The Battalion was relieved by 4/8th Sherwood-Foresters and proceed to Equancourt where it was under Canvas at V.16.a.61.	AKB.

Commandg 2/4 Leicestershire Regt

WAR DIARY 2/4th LEICESTERSHIRE REGT.
INTELLIGENCE SUMMARY
JUNE 1917

Army Form C. 2118.

(Erase heading not required.)

Instructions regarding War Diaries and Intelligence Summaries are contained in F.S. Regs., Part II. and the Staff Manual respectively. Title pages will be prepared in manuscript.

Hour, Date, Place	Summary of Events and Information	Remarks and references to Appendices
22.6.17 FEQUANCOURT V.16.a.6.1	Reinforcement draft of 40 other ranks arrived to CALAIS.	J.D.
22.6.17 do	2/Lt G. BOLUS reported for duty	J.D.
23.6.17 do	2/Lt P. WALDRON proceeded to FOUQUECOURT on Revolver course	J.D.
26.6.17 do	Major J.C. BAINES reported for duty to CALAIS.	J.D.
26.6.17 do	Capt BLUNT proceeded to FLIXECOURT on Infantry Company Commanders course Lieut L.B. ORCHARD proceeded to BOUCHON on sniping course	J.D.
26.6.17 do	2/Lt P. WALDRON returned to duty from revolver course	J.D.
29.6.17 do	Reinforcement draft of 6 other ranks arrived to CALAIS.	J.D.

Bowes
Major
Cmdg 2/4 Leicestershire Regt

SECRET

ORIGINAL

2/4 LEICESTERSHIRE REGT
Army Form C. 2118.

WAR DIARY
INTELLIGENCE SUMMARY.
(Erase heading not required.)

JULY 1917.

177/59

Hour, Date, Place	Summary of Events and Information	Remarks and references to Appendices
1/7/17. Q.10.d.3.7. Ref: map 57.C.S.E.	Battalion moved to Q.10.d.3.7. front line of left sector (ref: map 57.C.S.E.). 2 Coys in front line - 2 platoons front line - 2 platoons in support. B Coy in close support with 2 platoons in Ptolemayport.	J.D.
1/7/17. EQUANCOURT.	2/Lt M.S. HAINE + 2/Lt J.C. HUTCHINSON proceeded to Corive to FOUCAUCOURT	J.D.
1/7/17. EQUANCOURT.	2/Lt A.E. WAND proceeded to ENGLAND as instructor in bombing for 2 months.	J.D.
2/7/17. Q.10.d.3.7. Ref: map 57.C.S.E.	4 reinforcements ex CALAIS.	J.D.
3/7/17. Q.10.d.3.7. Ref: map 57.C.S.E.	Divl artillery and 3° Corps artillery bombard enemy Trenches and roads opposite our sector.	J.D.
4/7/17. Q.10.d.3.7. Ref: map 57.C.S.E.	Major J.C. BAINES proceeds on leave to ENGLAND (10 days)	J.D.
4/7/17. Q.10.d.3.7. Ref: map 57.C.S.E.	Major R.A. HENDERSON assumes command of Battalion. Capt A SILVER acted in command of	J.D.
4/7/17. Q.10.d.3.7. Ref: map 57.C.S.E.	3rd Corps Artillery bombards RIBECOURT - TRESCAULT ROAD	J.D.

C. G. Logan
Lt Col
Commdg 2/4 Leicestershire Regt

ORIGINAL 2/4 LEICESTERSHIRE REGT

SECRET

Army Form C. 2118.

JULY 1917.

WAR DIARY
INTELLIGENCE SUMMARY.
(Erase heading not required.)

Instructions regarding War Diaries and Intelligence Summaries are contained in F.S. Regs., Part II. and the Staff Manual respectively. Title pages will be prepared in manuscript.

Hour, Date, Place	Summary of Events and Information	Remarks and references to Appendices
5/7/17 B.10.d.3.7. Ref: 57.c.SE	Battalion relieved by 5th Leinsters in the Line. Battalion moved to METZ in support.	
5/7/17 B.10.d.3.7. Ref: map 57.c.SE	A/Lt Col Sir Iain COLQUHOUN Bt DSO took over command	
5/7/17 B.10.d.3.7. Ref: map 57.c.SE	2 men killed, 3 wounded	
5/7/17 METZ	Lieut E.B. OLIVER returned from leave.	
6/7/17 METZ	3 men wounded, one of whom died of wounds	
6/7/17 METZ	2/Lt H.J. PARTRIDGE reported for duty	
7/7/17 METZ	2 other ranks reported from C.C.S.	
8/7/17 METZ	2/Lt G.R. HODGKINS admitted to hospital	
10/7/17 METZ	Battalion relieved by 2/8 LONDON REGT.	
11/7/17 BARASTRE	Battalion moved to BARASTRE Camp O.16.d 2 other ranks reported from C.C.S.	
11/7/17 BARASTRE	2/Lt L.B. ORCHARD + several signallers have signalling course.	

Signed [signature]
Lt Col
Cmdg 2/4 Leicestershire Regt

ORIGINAL

SECRET

2/4 LEICESTERSHIRE REGT   Army Form C. 2118.

WAR DIARY
INTELLIGENCE SUMMARY.
(Erase heading not required.)

JULY 1917

Instructions regarding War Diaries and Intelligence Summaries are contained in F.S. Regs., Part II. and the Staff Manual respectively. Title pages will be prepared in manuscript.

Hour, Date, Place		Summary of Events and Information	Remarks and references to Appendices
12/7/17	BARASTRE	2/4 J.P. HODGKINS departed from hospital and proceeded on leave to ENGLAND.	92.
16/7/17	BARASTRE	2/Lt J.S. ROWLEY proceeded on leave to ENGLAND	92.
20/7/17	BARASTRE	CAPT WAITE proceeded on leave to ENGLAND	92.
21/7/17	BARASTRE	Divisional sports	92.
22/7/17	BARASTRE	4 Other ranks joined the Battalion	92.
24/7/17	BARASTRE	4 Other ranks sent to CALAIS Arrupt	92.
24/7/17	BARASTRE	CAPT R.SILVER proceed on leave ENGLAND	92.
25/7/17	BARASTRE	Divisional musketry meeting	92.
27/7/17	BARASTRE	DIVISIONAL TRAINING	92.
24/7/17	BARASTRE	(R.PT.) HENDE RSON proceeded on leave to ENGLAND.	92.
26/7/17	BARASTRE	2 Companies held Young at N.S.d. map. 57.C.S.W.	92.

Colenlaryn Lt.Col.
Cmdg 2/4 Leicestershire Regt.

ORIGINAL
2/4 LEICESTERSHIRE REGT
AUGUST 1917

SECRET

WAR DIARY or INTELLIGENCE SUMMARY.

(Erase heading not required.)

Army Form C. 2118.

Hour, Date, Place	Summary of Events and Information	Remarks and references to Appendices
BARASTRE 1-8-17 Sheet 57C D.16.d.Central	2/LTS SHAUL and ORCHARD proceeded on leave to ENGLAND Battalion continued Training	177/59/ 2.2.
" 2-8-17	2/LTS H.W. MILLER R.E.W. BECKETT and B.W.C. MAIN reported for duty with the Battalion – Bn Training	2.2.
" 3-8-17	CAPT N.S. WAITE reported for duty from leave	2.2.
" 6-8-17	CAPT A. SILVER reported for duty from leave – Bn Training	2.2.
" 6-8-17	CAPT F.G. SNAITH proceeded to ENGLAND on leave	2.2.
" 8-8-17	6 other ranks reinforcements reported – Bn Training	2.2.
" 9-8-17	2/LT P. WALDRON proceeded on leave to BOVES	3.3.
" 10-8-17	2/LT J. HARPY proceeded on leave to ENGLAND Bn Training	3.3.
" 10-8-17	CAPT R.A. FENDER S.N. reported from leave Brigade Training	3.2.
" 11-8-17	36 O.R. Reinforcements reported at CALAIS	
" 12-8-17	2/LT H.W. MILLER proceeded on course to WARLEY	4.2.
" 12-8-17	17 O.R. Reinforcements reported at CALAIS	
" 13-8-17	LT R.K. BLUNT and 2/LT E.C. SWAIN proceeded to ENGLAND on leave. – Bn Training	2.2.
" 14-8-17	2/LT A.E. SHAUL reported from leave	
" 14-8-17	2/LT H.B. THOMASON reported for duty – Bn Training	

Colquhoun Lt.Col
Comdg 2/4 LEICESTER REGT

SECRET

2/4 LEICESTERSHIRE REGT

Army Form C. 2118.

WAR DIARY or INTELLIGENCE SUMMARY.

(Erase heading not required.)

AUGUST 1917

Instructions regarding War Diaries and Intelligence Summaries are contained in F.S. Regs., Part II. and the Staff Manual respectively. Title pages will be prepared in manuscript.

Hour, Date, Place	Summary of Events and Information	Remarks and references to Appendices
BARASTRE 15-8-17	2/LT L.B. ORCHARD reports from leave - Bn Training	92
" 16-8-17	L.O.R. Reinforcements arrived ex CALAIS - Bn Training	92
" 17-8-17	CAPT. R.G. SNAITH returned from leave - Bn Training	92
" 18-8-17	2/LT H.G. PARTRIDGE reports from leave	92
" 19-8-17	2/LT A.G. RALEIGH proceeds to ENGLAND on leave	92
" 19-8-17	2/LT C.D. BROWN reports for duty with the Battalion	92
" 20-8-17	Bn Training. Reinforcements arrived ex CALAIS	92
" 21-8-17	Inspection of recent drafts by G.O.C. Division	22
" 22-8-17	- Bn Training	22
" 22-8-17	2/LT T.C. SMITH proceeds to ENGLAND on leave	92
" 22-8-17	Battalion moved from BARASTRE to SENLIS by route march and bus	92
SENLIS 23-8-17 (Hucis7D P10.d.0.4.)	2/LT SHARP reports from leave	92
" 24-8-17	2/LT M.J. HAINE admitted to hospital	92
" 25-8-17	Bn Training	
" 26-8-17	2/LT J.C. HUTCHINSON proceeds to ENGLAND on leave	92
" 27-8-17	2/LT H.W. MILLIER reports from course - Bn Training	

10 Colquhoun, Lt.Col.
Cmdg 2/4 LEICESTER SHIRE REGT

SECRET   2/4 LEICESTERSHIRE REGT   Army Form C. 2118.

AUGUST 1917

WAR DIARY
or
INTELLIGENCE SUMMARY.
(Erase heading not required.)

Instructions regarding War Diaries and Intelligence
Summaries are contained in F.S. Regs., Part II.
and the Staff Manual respectively. Title pages
will be prepared in manuscript.

Hour, Date, Place	Summary of Events and Information	Remarks and references to Appendices
SENLIS 27-8-17.	2/LT E.G. SWAIN reports from Home Bn Training	J.D.
" 28-8-17		J.D.
" 30-8-17	2/LTs W.R SOWTER and C.H CROSS proceeded to ENGLAND	J.D.
" 30-8-17.	on leave	
	CAPT R.A. HENDERSON, proceeded on leave to LE TOUQUET.	J.D.
" 31-8-17	9 O.R. Reinforcements reported to CALAIS	J.D.
" 31-8-17	Battalion moved from SENLIS to NINJWENHOEK	
	& WINNEZEELE. Scheme 27.9.4.d.6.5.	J.D.
" 31-8-17	2/LT A.G. RALEIGH reported from leave	

Colquhoun Lt. Col
Cmdg 2/4 LEICESTERSHIRE REGT

SECRET 2/4 LEICESTERSHIRE Army Form C.2118.

SEPTR 1917 177/59

WAR DIARY
INTELLIGENCE SUMMARY.
(Erase heading not required.)

Instructions regarding War Diaries and Intelligence Summaries are contained in F.S. Regs., Part II. and the Staff Manual respectively. Title pages will be prepared in manuscript.

Hour, Date, Place	Summary of Events and Information	Remarks and references to Appendices
VINNEZEELE 1-9-17. Jud 6.5 (Sheet 27 N.E.)	Battalion Training ~~D~~ E.S.	98.
2-9-17	2/Lt M.J. HAINE transferred to ENGLAND on 2/Lt V.C. LOWRY transferred to ENGLAND on leave	98.
do 3-9-17	Training. 2/Lt J.C. Smith returned from leave	98.
do 4-9-17	2/Lt A.F COOK reported for duty	98.
do 6-9-17	Training. 2/Lt J.E. HUTCHINSON returned from leave	98.
do 7-9-17	2/Lt H.W JAYLOR proceeded on leave to ENGLAND Training.	98.
do 8-9-17	2/Lt T.B. MASTERS reported for duty 2/Lt A.B. GOULD reported for duty	98.
do 9-9-17	2/Lt R.J. WIDDOWSON reported for duty	98.

(9.20.6) W 3332—1107 100,000 10/13 HWV Forms/C. 2118/10

2/4 LEICESTERSHIRE REGT

SECRET

Army Form C. 2118.

Sept 1917

WAR DIARY
or
INTELLIGENCE SUMMARY.
(Erase heading not required.)

Instructions regarding War Diaries and Intelligence
Summaries are contained in F.S. Regs., Part II.
and the Staff Manual respectively. Title pages
will be prepared in manuscript.

Hour, Date, Place		Summary of Events and Information	Remarks and references to Appendices
WINNEZEELE	9-9-17.	2/Lt C.H. CROSS and W.R. SOWTER returned from leave.	33.
J.U.2.6.5			
do	10-9-17.	Training	
		CAPT H.A. MACMILLAN returned from leave	33
do	15-9-17	CAPT. F. DICKINSON and Lt. F. Arm. & WITHERS proceeded	
		on leave to ENGLAND	
do	17-9-17	2/Lt H.W. TAYLOR returned from leave	33.
do	20-9-17.	Battalion moved to neighbourhood of POPERINGHE	33.
		Map ref. L.9.6.55.	
D.20.a.5.5	24-9-17.	Battalion moved to YPRES in Motor Lorries in support	33
(Pt CHAMPSTREET MAP		to STAFFORD Brigade. MAP Ref. D.20.a.5.5.	
attached)		Relief carried out at 6.15pm and was carried out by ???	
		without casualties	
		Capt. F. DICKINSON and Lt. Young Withers returned from	33
		leave	
do	25-9-17.	Battalion moved dispositions as follows:-	

Signed ??? ???
Cmdg 2/4 Leic Regt.

(9 29 6) W 3332-1107 100,000 10/13 H W V Forms/C. 2118/10

SECRET

2/4 LEICESTERSHIRE REGT

WAR DIARY or INTELLIGENCE SUMMARY

Army Form C. 2118.

Sept 1917

Hour, Date, Place	Summary of Events and Information	Remarks and references to Appendices
D30.a.6.5 25-9-17	2 Companies holding front line, one Coy in the Maa, one French Coy carrying party. (See operation orders attached)	A.8.
do 26-9-17	At 5.15 am our preliminary bombardment started. At 5.50 am our barrage opened and leading waves of the C & D Coys went over the top to their tapes at a distance of 100 yds. At 6.10 the 2/5 Lincolns moved up through our rear up in support. At 10 am following barrage moved by telephone preparing satisfactorily. At 6.30 am our first German prisoners began to come in helping many of our wounded.	

72 I cave Stephen Nicol
andy 2/4 Lei Regt

SECRET

2/4 LEICESTER SH Army Form C. 2118.
Sept 1917

WAR DIARY
or
INTELLIGENCE SUMMARY.
(Erase heading not required.)

Instructions regarding War Diaries and Intelligence Summaries are contained in F.S. Regs., Part II. and the Staff Manual respectively. Title pages will be prepared in manuscript.

Hour, Date, Place	Summary of Events and Information	Remarks and references to Appendices
D.20.a.5.5 26-9-17.	At 6.50 am following murky dawn. First objective taken eventually light consolidation proceeding. Consolidation proceeded with subsequent much rifle & m.g. fire, we found all enemy unprotected as we are by our artillery. We had 15 to 20 casualties up to our right flank. Our casualties up to now were approximately 70 including Capt A. SILVER 2/4 D.E. SMITH 11.30 am news came through that the LINCOLNS had taken all objectives & are now consolidating. Our Barrage fire continued practically all the day with an intensity hitherto unprecedented. Our guns are also shelling the whole area continuously and our casualties mounted.	J.D. F. Goshen-Hall Lt/Col. 2/4 Leic R.

SECRET

2/4 LEICESTERSHIRE REGT

Army Form C. 2118.

SEPTR 1917

WAR DIARY
or
INTELLIGENCE SUMMARY.
(Erase heading not required.)

Hour, Date, Place	Summary of Events and Information	Remarks and references to Appendices
D.20.a.6.5 26-9-17.	Bn HQrs moved to D.20.a.6.5. 6.30 pm owing to a misunderstanding certain troops holding front trenches in our Bigeon sector moved back & withdrew this unfortunately produced a move or two forced withdrawal along the whole front although very few men of this Battalion left the trenches. By the efforts of Officers the situation was retrieved as the old British front line thus a general advance commenced. The trench system was all reoccupied & reorganisation of parties commenced. Bn HQ 7.45 p.m. During the day we captured 5 machine guns and 2 hours prisoners.	70
do 27-9-17.	The Battalion relieved me in our sector by 2/5th Lincolns on the line and extending our frontage 300 yards.	by Telephone Cards a/4 Leics Regt

WAR DIARY or INTELLIGENCE SUMMARY

2/4 LEICESTERSHIRE REGT
Army Form C. 2118.
SEPTR 1917

Place	Hour, Date	Summary of Events and Information	Remarks and references to Appendices
D.20.a.5.5	28-9-17	During the evening the Germans counter attacked in our right but failed to penetrate our lines. Artillery was very active during the day on both sides	
do	29-9-17	The morning was very quiet on both sides. At 6 p.m. a very heavy German barrage started which continued till 7.30	S.D.
do	30-9-17	At 4.30 a.m. the Germans again opened a heavy barrage which continued for 2 hours. Nothing occurred after. Battalion was relieved in the line by the NEW ZEALANDERS and moved to Cail Reserve. During our tour in the line we had the following casualties. Officers Killed 2/Lt B.P. HODGKINS. 2/Lt B. THOMAS. OR Wounded. Capt A. SILVER 2/Lt A.B. GOULD 2/Lt A. FLOOR 2/Lt J.C. SMITH 2/Lt H. NEWBOLD at Duty OR Killed 28 Wounded 147 Missing	S.D.

2/4th LEICESTERSHIRE REGIMENT.   24. 9. 17

OPERATION ORDERS.
Ref. Gravenstafel Map.

1. The 59th Division will attack with two Brigades, the 177th on the right and the 178th on the left. Each Brigade will attack with 2 Bns. in the front line.
   The 176th Brigade will send 1 Bn. to each of the 177th and 178th Brigades. The remaining two Bns. of the 176th Brigade will be in Divisional Reserve in the old British front line.

2. The attached map shows (1) inter-Divisional and Bde: and Bn. boundaries, (2) Certain artillery barrage lines, (3) Strong points to be constructed.

3. The artillery barrages show the various objectives of each Brigade. The barrage on green line reaches it at plus 18 minutes and lifts plus 38.
   The barrage on the red line reaches it at plus 56 minutes and lifts plus 105.
   The barrage on blue line reaches it at plus 145 minutes and lifts plus 185.
   The barrage on yellow line reaches it at plus 205.

4. The artillery barrage will be put down at Zero 150 yards on front of our forming up line. It will move in lifts of 50 yards at the following rates.
   100 yards in 4 minutes for the first 200 yards.
   Then 100 yards in 6 minutes up to red line.
   After the red line 100 yards in 8 minutes.

   If possible a smoke barrage will be placed along HANEBEEK VALLEY from BOURDEAUX FARM to RIVERSIDE.

5. In front of Artillery barrage there will be a M.G. barrage of 40 guns.
   In addition arrangements will be made for a S.O.S. barrage in front of final objective.
   The 2/4th Leicesters have at their disposal 2 guns of the M.G. Coy: These will form up with support Coy: (B Coy:) and occupy.

6. Plan of attack will be as follows:-
   The 2/4th Leicesters will attack on a two company frontage. A Coy: on the left, D Coy: on the right, B Coy: in support, and C Coy: in reserve.
   The battalion frontage is 480 yards, each front line Coy: will attack on a frontage of 240 yards.
   (b) The 2/5th Leicesters will be on the left of A Coy: and a Bnn of the 175th Bde on the right of D Coy:
   (c) At Zero hour the 2/4th Leicesters will advance position of assembly and gain a line 100 yds. short of red barrage line (1st objective). Under cover of the 49 minutes pause in advance of barrage they will reorganize and consolidate occupying any captured strong points and forming defensive flank if necessary.
   (d) At Zero plus 105 minutes the 2/4th Lincolns will pass through 2/4th Leicesters and gain and consolidate a line 100 yards short of blue barrage line (2nd objective).
   (e) At Zero plus 185 minutes the 2/4th Lincolns will advance and gain and consolidate a line 100 yds. short of yellow barrage (final objective).

7. (1). "D" Coy: will detail the following men to capture the following places.
   (a) One section to capture dug-out on extreme right flank about 75 yards from starting point.
   (b) One platoon to capture concrete emplacement at cross roads D.20.d.5.9. about 400 yds from starting point.
(2) "A" Coy: will detail the following men to capture the following points:-
   (a) One platoon to take Tulip cottages if occupied.
   (b) One platoon to capture the 3 concrete emplacements in a group at D.20.b.4.5

8. The most advanced troops will be prepared to light flares and signal with Watson fans when they are called for by the contact aeroplane.

9. Companies will repulse by immediate attack any hostile counter-attacks which may penetrate our line.

10. Bn. Hqrs: will be notified later.
R.A.P. at POMMERN CASTLE.

F.Dickinson, Capt: & Adjt:

2/4th Leicestershire Regt:

SECRET APPENDIX to WAR DIARY SEPT 1917
2/4 LEICESTERSHIRE REGT.
DETAILED ACCOUNT OF OPERATIONS
from 24/9/17 to 30/9/17

On the 24th Sept 1917 the Battalion moved
from the neighbourhood of POPERINGHE up
to YPRES north sector in support to the
Stafford Brigade. MAP Ref: Gravenstafel D.20.a & 5.
The Battalion relieved the Staffords in the line
that night. The relief started at 8pm and was
complete by 1am without casualties. Our
dispositions were as follows:- 2 Companies holding
the front line, one Company in the rear. The
4th Coy was used as a carrying party (see
Bn operation orders attached to War Diary). Our
Headquarters were established in a trench near
BEMTRE CORNER.

Nothing of incident had occurred up to this
point and the artillery on both sides was
fairly quiet.

At 5.15am our preliminary bombardment
commenced and lasted with great intensity
until 5.50am. The german artillery replied
vigorously all the time but was generally
speaking not severe.

At 5.50am our barrage opened and the
leading waves of C & D Companies went over
the top to time, followed by B Coy at a distance
of 100 yards.

At 6.10am we received the first information
of the progress of the attack on the following

telephone message "half way to first objective
casualties light progressing satisfactorily"
About this time the 2nd LINCOLNS crossed
our front line trench and went up in
support.

At 6.30 am the first of the German prisoners
began to come in and many of them were
seen to be helping our own wounded
along to the dressing station.

News of the capture of the first objective
was received by phone at 6.50 am in the
following message "First objective taken
casualties light consolidation proceeding"
The consolidation of our first objective was
continued under rather heavy shell fire
but proceeded very satisfactorily. Our leading
waves found all the enemy concrete
emplacements smashed in by our artillery
fire, and a great many enemy dead near
by.

B Coy who were following up in rear
of our leading waves now took up a
defensive position to our right flank.

Up to the time of taking the first
objective our casualties were approximately
70 including two Officers Capt H Selim
and 2/Lt T.C Smith.

The Artillery on both sides had now

reached a great intensity but nothing of
incident happened until 11.30 a.m. when
news was received at HQrs that the Divisions
had taken all their objectives and were
consolidating their positions.

Shortly after this our telephone lines
were cut by shell fire. Lieut Orchard (to
whom the whole credit of originally
laying the lines under the heaviest shell
fire is due) went forward with his linesmen
and repaired the damage, thus re-establishing
communication with the front. It also
brought us information that during the
advance to the first objective a party
of German snipers for some time held up
the advance of A Coy until Capt Silva went
forward on his own and having discovered
where they were hidden shot three of them
himself thus enabling the advance
to continue, although he himself was
wounded.

Our Barrage fire continued practically
all the day with an intensity hitherto
unprecedented. The Germans also shelled
the whole area continuously thus making
the work of establishing communication
very difficult. On several occasions when it
was impossible to mend the wires, 2/Lt
Orchard went through the German and
our own barrage bringing back most

(3)

valuable information to HQrs.

Our Headquarters moved to D.20.a.8.5 after the taking of the first objective and remained there for the rest of the attack.

At about 6.30 pm that night owing to a misunderstanding certain troops holding the front line trenches in our Brigade sector were seen to withdraw. This unfortunately produced a more or less general retirement along the whole front, although very few men of this Battalion left the trenches. By the efforts of the officers present the retirement was stopped at the old British front line and a general advance commenced. The trench system was all reoccupied and reorganisation of various units proceeded with by 7.45pm

During the day we captured 5 machine guns two trench mortars and about 80 prisoners.

The remainder of the night was comparatively quiet except for a certain amount of artillery fire on both sides.

The morning of the 27th was exceptionally quiet and it was quite possible to go round the entire system without any trouble. In the evening the Battalion relieved the 2nd & 5th LINCOLNS in the line and extended the

(4)

frontage 300 yards to the right. The relief
passed off without incident and was
complete by 2.am.

During the evening of the 28th Germans
counter attacked on the 3rd Divisional
frontage on our right but failed to
penetrate our barrage which was very
intense.

The morning of the 29th was very quiet
on both sides, and it appeared that the
Germans had withdrawn some of his
heavy guns and was registering again
from his new positions.

At 6 pm in the evening he started
a heavy bombardment which continued
till 7.30 pm when things quietened
down for the rest of the night. But at
4.30 am on the 30th he commenced
another heavy bombardment both of the
front line and back areas. our heavies
replied and the bombardment ceased
at 6.30 am.

The rest of the day was quiet
but towards evening his artillery
livened up but did not reach any
degree of intensity.

At 7 pm the Battalion was relieved

(5)

in the line by the NEW ZEALANDERS and moved to calf Reserve. The relief was complete by 9.15 p.m.

During the Battalions tour in the line we had the following casualties.

Officers Killed

2/Lt J.P. Hodgkins — 2/Lt Thomasson

Officers wounded

Capt H. SILVER — 2/Lt A.B. GOULD — 2/Lt A.F. COOK
2/Lt T.C. Smith

Officers wounded at duty

Capt. E.G. SNAITH
 „   F. DICKINSON
 „   H.A. MACMILLAN

Other Ranks Killed

28

Other Ranks wounded missing

147

In the field
5/10/17.

Iain Colquhoun
Lt Col
Cmdg 2/4 Leic Regt.

ORIGINAL

SECRET Army Form C. 2118.

Instructions regarding War Diaries and Intelligence Summaries are contained in F.S. Regs., Part II. and the Staff Manual respectively. Title pages will be prepared in manuscript.

WAR DIARY 2/4 Leicestershire Regt.
INTELLIGENCE SUMMARY
(Erase heading not required.)

OCTOBER 1917   Vol 9

Place	Date	Hour	Summary of Events and Information	Remarks and references to Appendices
VLAMERTINGHE	1.10.17	5.30 PM	Battn. moved from CAMP RESERVE by march route at 5.30 PM to VLAMERTINGHE. Arrived casualties arrived at Bull Ring	Ref- 28 men from
do	2.10.17	11 AM	Bn. moved from Vlamertinghe at 11 AM to THIENNES by train arriving at 6 PM. Remained 4 nights. Interior economy & Reorganisation of Bn. daily.	W.R.S.
				W.R.S.
THIENNES	6.10.17	9 AM	Bn. moved from Thiennes to BEAUMETZ by Buses & march route. C & D Coys march route to WITTERNESSE then by Bus & Art. B. Coys by Bus to WITTERNESSE then by march route	W.R.S. W.R.S.
BEAUMETZ	8.10.17		Training. Reorganising. Lieut. G.B. OLIVER to hospital.	W.R.S.
THIENNES	4.10.17		2 Lts. J. RICHMOND. J.A.E. SPRINGATE. A.E. JEFFRIES. J.C. BRUCE. H.C. BAKER. G. STEVENSON + 106 OR reported for duty	W.R.S. W.R.S.
BEAUMETZ	9.10.17		Bn. training. Lt. Col. Sir IAIN COLQUHOUN Bt. D.S.O. proceeded on leave	W.R.S.
do	10.10.17	8.30 AM	Bn. moved from BEAUMETZ to DIEVAL arriving 3 PM. Ref Map. HAZEBROUCK B.M.H.Q. 1.F.4.2	W.R.S.
DIEVAL	11.10.17	12.15 PM	Bn. moved from DIEVAL to HOUDAIN arriving abt 2.20 PM. Bn. HQ 213 Rue de Bourdin	W.R.S.
HOUDAIN	12.10.17	9.45 AM	Bn. moved from HOUDAIN to COUPIGNY SERVINS arriving at 12.15 PM.	W.R.S.

2/4 Leicestershire Regt.

Army Form C. 2118.

1st Leicestershire Regt

WAR DIARY
INTELLIGENCE SUMMARY.
(Erase heading not required.)

SECRET
Instructions regarding War Diaries and Intelligence Summaries are contained in F.S. Regs., Part II. and the Staff Manual respectively. Title pages will be prepared in manuscript.

Place	Date	Hour	Summary of Events and Information	Remarks and references to Appendices
GOUY SERVINS	13/10/17	9:45AM	Bn moved to SOUCHEZ at 9:15AM arrived. Huts evacuated 5:20P.M.	WRS
			Bn moved up into support in AVION SECTOR relieving 13th Canadian Bn. Disposition Coy Right Front. D Coy Right Centre. B Coy Left Centre. B Coy Left Front. Relief completed 11:40P.M. Bn H.Q. Ref Map. LENS CANAL S6 central.	WRS
LENS CANAL S6 central	14/10/17		Quiet. Nothing to report.	WRS
"	15/10/17	4 AM	Inspected by R.E.'s on our Left.	WRS
"	16/10/17		Nothing to report.	WRS
"	17/10/17		Bn relieved 5th Leicesters in the Bute Right Sub-Sector. Dispositions A Coy Right. D Coy Left. B Coy Support. C Coy Reserve. Relief complete 10:30P.M. Bn HQ LENS CANAL T3 a.u.2. Ref M.S.	WRS
LENS CANAL T3 a.u.2.	18/10/17		Quiet. Nothing to report. (Patrols report as usual.)	WRS
"	19/10/17		Quiet. Nothing to report.	WRS
"	20/10/17		Quiet. Nothing to report.	WRS
"	21/10/17		Enemy put up a Barrage on our front & support Lines at 5:30P.M. until 6:30P.M. Retaliation asked for, & SOS was sent up. Their Batteries neutralised at 6:30P.M.	WRS
"	22/10/17	2AM	Bn relieved by 2/5 Sherwoods. Bn moved to Bn reserve at GOUY SERVINS by Coys from 2:00 to Decauville Rly. Landed at GOUY SERVINS by the Leicestershire Regt.	WRS

D. D. & L., London, E.C. (A5852) Wt. W803/M1672 350,000 4/17 Forms/C/2118/4 Sch. 52a.

SECRET

WAR DIARY
or
INTELLIGENCE SUMMARY
(Erase heading not required.)

Army Form C. 2118.

2/4 Lincolnshire Rgt.

Place	Date	Hour	Summary of Events and Information	Remarks and references to Appendices
GOUY SERVINS	23.10.17		Bn. Training. 2nd Lt. F. DICKINSON admitted to hospital	WD
"	24.10.17		Bn. Training. Lt. Col. Sir IAN COLQUHOUN Bt. D.S.O. returned from leave	WD
"	25.10.17		Bn. Training. 2nd Lt. G.H. BAKER proceeded on Lewis gun course	WD
"	26.10.17		Bn. Training. 2nd Lt. H.W. MILLER reported for duty from hospital	WD
"	27.10.17		Bn. Training	WD
"	28.10.17		Bn. Training	WD
"	29.10.17	5 PM	Bn. moved to LIEVIN by Decauville Rly. relieving 2/5 South Staffordshire Rgt. in reserve in the Right Sub Sector. Supt. G.B. OLIVER returned from hospital	WD
LIEVIN M.27.b.50.30			Relief completed 7.00 PM. Bn. H.Q. Refugees LENS 36.C.S.W.1. M.27.b.50.30.	WD
"	30.10.17		Quiet nothing to report	WD
"	31.10.17		Quiet nothing to report	WD

Ian Colquhoun Lt. Col.
Comdg 2/4 Lincolnshire Rgt.

Patrol Report

A patrol of 1 NCO & 2 men proceeded at 8am from first line at point N32.c.25.80 along Rly embankment with object of reconnoitre position at N33.a.4.0. They proceeded along Rly bank & railway without incident for a distance of 250x at no firing having been received. What was evidently a m.g. fired about 54 rpds this appeared to be about 100 yds across the railway. At this point he returned & he heard sounds of shooting going on at about N33.a.4.0 evidently an enemy party at work under the active by listening & T.M.B opened at those firing ending of shells onto the M.G.E by sent this proved that the enemy is well established at this point. It would appear however that the first is not this crater but clearly to the right.
NATURE OF GROUND patrolled. At a distance of 100x from bank L.G. sat at about N33.c.25.80 we crossed rails away and the culture around

embankment, this is one almost
15' high. Further along, by Railway
to stream walls, barn iron, Timber
etc such as used in construction
of dug outs. About 330x from point
N 33 c.25.80 the embankment
ends and Railway runs
almost parallel to ground. The
patrol worked towards 33 c 30x
from this point. Owing to nature
of ground described above it
would be a simple matter for
the Enemy to send a small
patrol along Railway to within
100x of our post at N 33 c. 25.80
Beyond this point he would
be bound to be discovered.
The Patrol returned at 12.30 am
point of N- entering line N.33.c.25.80

2. A patrol of 1 officer 1 NCO & 3 men.
proceeded at 7.30 pm from our
lines at point N 33.c.25.80 Proceeded
along Embankment to hedge
running East from point
N 33.c.40.80 with Object of
providing covering fire to
No.1. patrol & to capture any

prisoners. No enemy were seen + no movement heard. They report he noted flares were sent up from the same position as last night. The patrol returned as soon as they heard hostile whistle returning. They reached our lines about 12.30 am at point N33C.2.5.5

3. A patrol of 1 N.C.O. + 5 men + left our front line N.6. at bng at point N33C.1.9. to reconnoitre ground from N33a.3.2. to N33.6.0. & as far as a row of houses N.E. of the top reference, & were to [?] to go forward if & get in touch with enemy. They proceeded along [?] to holding out at point N33a.2.2. + to [?] B.4 about now 25° ahead as L.P. + ready by night for covering fire if necessary. The patrol proceeded forward in a northerly direction. They almost immediately ran into water + marshy ground. They patrolled N.N.W. along line on about 200°. [?] the water did not wish but to

snipers to the rear, the patrol came
back to their covering party. They
then worked along the wire
towards Railway. They found
the wire ended about 25* from
Railway but the ground between
this point & Railway was too
marshy to permit them going
forward. They then proceeded to
work back to our front line
when about 60* NE of point
N.33.c.1.7 three of our shrapnel shells
evidently directed at our front
line fell short. One burst
about 2* to left of patrol
wounding one man. The others
escaped injury. No enemy
was seen or movement heard.
Patrol returned 2.30 p.m. to
point N.33.c.1.7

4. A patrol consisting of 1 Officer
  & 30 other ranks left our line at
  N.33.d.40.25 to reconnoitre as
  far as possible N.33.b central
  discover enemy outposts and
  if possible to secure a prisoner.
  Patrol moved from our lines

Patrol went to [Hudson?] Posts
Road of [?] [?] good
[?] [?] N32 [?].
About 30° [?] the [?] [?] of
N[?] [?] a [?] [?]
[?] [?] N [?] [?]
[?] of [?] were found to
be [?] [?] [?] [?]
found [?] to be [?]
[?] to a large [?]
of [?] [?] [?] a very bad
ground [almost?] a [?]
[?] [?] [?] [?] [?] [?]
were [?] [?] [?] [?] [?]
out looking [?] [?]
to work up closer [?]
with out [?] [?]
[?] [?] [?] [?] [?] [?]
closer [?] [?] [?] [?]
[?] [?] where a large
quantity of [?] [?]
was [?] on both sides
of road. No [?] enemy post
was discovered. [?] [?]
that the enemy [?] [?] [?]
is fairly strongly held [?] [?]
a [?] going on [?] [?] [?]
[?] & sounds [?] [?] [?] [?]
[?] boards [?] [?]

CONFIDENTIAL / ORIGINAL

SECRET Army Form C. 2118.

WAR DIARY
2/4 LEICESTERSHIRE REGT
INTELLIGENCE SUMMARY
NOVR. 1917

Vol 10

Place	Date	Hour	Summary of Events and Information	Remarks and references to Appendices
LIEVIN M27 b & 5	1st		Quiet - nothing to report	with
"	2		Quiet - nothing to report	with
"	3		Quiet - nothing to report	with
"	4		Quiet - nothing to report	with
"	5		Quiet - nothing to report	with
"	6		Bn relieved 2/5 London Regt in the night - reliefs of Left B/n Front relay complete at 2.40 AM 7-11-17. Bn HQ M30a&8. Map 36c	with
M30a&8	7		Quiet - nothing to report	with
"	8		Quiet - nothing to report	with
"	9		Enemy T.M. shelled our front line our right	with
"	10		Two Patrols went out from our front line. Patrol reports attached	with
"	11		One Patrol went out from our front line. Patrol report attached	with
"	12		Quiet - nothing to report	with
"	13		Quiet - nothing to report	with

C. Stephens Lt-Col
Cmdg 2/4th Leicestershire Regt

SECRET

WAR DIARY
or
INTELLIGENCE SUMMARY

Army Form C. 2118
2/4 LEICESTERSHIRE REGT
NOVEMBER

(Erase heading not required.)

Instructions regarding War Diaries and Intelligence Summaries are contained in F. S. Regs., Part II. and the Staff Manual respectively. Title pages will be prepared in manuscript.

Place	Date	Hour	Summary of Events and Information	Remarks and references to Appendices
M30 a 48	14		Quiet - nothing to report - Bn was relieved by 3rd Glowestershire Bn Relief complete 11.9 AM	WR.B
SOUCHEZ S8a central	15	11 AM	Bn moved to BOUCHEZ CAMP by March route. Bn HQ S8a central Map 36G	WR.B
CHATEAU DE LA HAIE	16		Bn moved by march route to CHATEAU DE LA HAIE. Bn training. Open Warfare.	WR.B WR.B
"	17	1.17 PM	Bn moved to HAUTEVILLE by march route via VILLERS-AUX-BOIS. — HAUTE-AVESNES — HARBARCQ — LATTRE ST-QUENTIN. Bn arrived 6.45 PM Bn HQ. J35 c.8.8. Ref Map Sheet 57 C	WR.B WR.B
HAUTEVILLE J35 c 8.8	18		Bn relief	WR.B WR.B
"	19	4.10 PM	Bn moved by march route to BAILLEULVAL arriving at 6.15 PM Bn HQ.	WR.B WR.B
BAILLEULVAL 4 H.65.65	20		Bn Training	WR.B WR.B
"	21	10.30 PM	Bn moved by march route to ACHIET-LE-PETIT arriving at 3.45 AM 22-11-17 Bn H.Q. 5.I.8.5 Map LENS 11	WR.B WR.B
ACHIET LE PETIT 5.I.8.5	22		Bn relief	WR.B WR.B

T. Colquhoun Lt Col
Comdg 2/4 Leicestershire Rgt.

SECRET

WAR DIARY
of
INTELLIGENCE SUMMARY
(Erase heading not required.)

2/4 Leicestershire Regt
November.

Army Form C. 2118.

Place	Date	Hour	Summary of Events and Information	Remarks and references to Appendices
ACHIET LE PETIT 57.8.5.	23	3.15 A.M.	Bn moved by march route ACHIET-LE-GRAND arriving 4.30 A.M. Bn moved by train to FINS arriving 12.30 P.M. & encamped in DESSART WOOD Map reference Q1d 3.8 Map 57C.	W.D.S.
DESSART WOOD Q1d.3.8.	24		Bn rested	W.D.S.
"	25		Bn rested	W.D.S.
"	26		Bn training	W.R.S.
"	27	12.0 P.M.	Bn moved by march route to FLESQUIERES arriving 5.30 P.M. Bn H.Q. K18.c.74 Map 57C relieving 3rd Grenadier Guards 12 Div.	W.D.R.
FLESQUIERES K15.C.7.4	28	7.30 P.M.	Bn moved by march route to LA JUSTICE Bn H.Q. L2.c.8.1. Map 57 C.	W.D.R.
LA JUSTICE L2.C.8.1	29		Guards in Bde Reserve. Nothing to report.	W.D.R.
"	30	8.40 A.M.	Artillery Heavy Bombardment by the enemy S.O.S. showed from our front line. Enemy attacked on both flanks. Bn moved to Support and Counter attacked & wounded W.D.R.	W.D.R.

Tim Ashby
Lt-Col
Cmdg 2/4 Leicestershire Regt.

Patrol Report

10.11.17

A Patrol of 1 NCO + 2 men left
704 Post N20 c 1 3 for a cottage
at N20 c 15.40 which is occupied
by the enemy.
The approach was very difficult
being over fallen houses & timber,
& it was difficult to get far
without making a noise. The
NCO advanced alone being
covered by the other 2 men.
The ordinary approach to the
cottage is from the N. side
which is covered by MG.
The NCO got into the cottage of
which only one wall remains
& found a grating through the
bricks from which a very
light was fired. The house is
apparently not occupied but
is connected from dug outs.
The NCO was unable to find in the
dark any approach to this house
& returned later to the same
starting point.

Patrol Report

10.11.17

A Patrol of 1 Officer & 4 OR proceeded from N.20.a.15.05 to N.20.a.25.05 at 5.0 a.m.

No signs of the enemy were seen or heard & patrol was obliged to return at 6.0 am owing to the light

Patrol Report

11.11.17

1. Officer + 4 O.R. left No 18 post N 30 a 25 30 to search house opposite the sheet supposed to be in Bosche hands.

The Patrol left the cellar of No 18 post at 5.40 pm through a hole in the wall + passed into the next door cellar. From there a shaft ran down at a steep incline under the road at the end of which steps led up to the street. On the right were 6 bunks let in the wall. To the left on going down two steps was found a passage with tables + chairs, + some bread etc on the table. The right of this passage was a series of bunks in two tiers along the wall. After about 30 yards there was a door which led to a passage to the right, at the end was a room very well furnished bed, stove, plush chairs mirror etc. There were dog bunks along the passage leading to this room. At the end was another door + passage at right angles with 2 exits up to the road.

ORIGINAL

SECRET

Army Form C. 2118.

WAR DIARY
INTELLIGENCE SUMMARY
(Erase heading not required.)

2/4 LEICESTERSHIRE RGT
DECEMBER

Place	Date	Hour	Summary of Events and Information	Remarks and references to Appendices
LA JUSTICE L2c 81.57C	1.		Bn relieved 2/6 N. Staffs Rgt & 2/6 S. Staffs Rgt in the front & support lines of the Left Sub-Sector. Relief complete 12.30 AM Bn HQ Q13 c 8.2. Reference map 57C.	
BOURLON WOOD F.13 c 8.2	2.		Enemy artillery active on our front & support line from 3.30 PM to 6.30 PM	N.T.R.
			Bn HQ moved to F.13 d 6.7. 57C.	N.T.R.
F.13 d 6.7	3.		Bn relieved by 2/4 Lines Rgt in the Left front line relief complete 12.30 AM Bn moved into support Bn HQ F.13 c 8.2. Sheet 57C. Enemy put down heavy Gas & HE bombardment between 8.30 PM & 4.30 AM. 2 Lt Richardson wounded Gas.	N.T.R.
F.13 c 8.2	4.	10 PM	Bn worked to Improved trenches in K 35.b (Over the Hindenburg Line) Bn HQ I.35 b 4.5 4 D Sheet 57C. 2/Lt B. Beckett proceeded on leave 15 England.	N.T.R. N.T.R.
K.35 b.4.5.40	5.		Bn relieved	N.T.R. N.T.R.
"	6.		In the shed. Leaving & Working parties supplied. Lieut North RAMC to hospital sick. Enemy attacked from Bourlon Wood to FONTAINE. Bn stood to from 2.30 PM to 5 PM. 2/Lt B. Beckett attack repulsed by artillery fire	N.T.R. certified

for 2/4 Leicestershire Rgt.

SECRET.

WAR DIARY
of
2/4 LEICESTERSHIRE RGT
INTELLIGENCE SUMMARY.
DECEMBER.

Army Form C. 2118.

Place	Date	Hour	Summary of Events and Information	Remarks and references to Appendices
K35.b.45.0.	7	9 A.M.	Bn working on the Hindenburg support	nil
"	8	9 "	Bn working on Hindenburg support	nil
"	9	9 "	Bn working on the Hindenburg support. 2/Lt Partridge sick to Hospital	nil
"	10		Bn relieved by 2/7 Sherwoods. Bn moved by march route to TRESCAULT. Bn HQ Q.ad.32. 57.C.	nil
Q.ad.32.	11	8 A.M.	Working parties	nil
"	12	"	Working parties	nil
"	13	"	Working parties. Capt. MacMillan reporting for duty	nil
"	14	"	Working parties. Bn relieved by 2/5 Lincolns Regt. Bn moved by march route to LECHELLE CAMP arriving 4.30 P.M. Bn H.Q. EF P.25.b.45.50. 57.C.	nil
LECHELLE P.25.b.45.50	15		Bn rested	nil
	16		Bn moved to BERTINCOURT by march route. Capt Selous reporting for duty P.7.c.8.8. 57.C.	nil

T Clephan Lt. Col.
Comdg 2/4 Leicestershire Regt.

SECRET.

WAR DIARY
or
INTELLIGENCE SUMMARY.
(Erase heading not required.)

Army Form C. 2118.

2/4 LEICESTERSHIRE R/67.
DECEMBER.

Instructions regarding War Diaries and Intelligence Summaries are contained in F. S. Regs., Part II. and the Staff Manual respectively. Title pages will be prepared in manuscript.

Place	Date	Hour	Summary of Events and Information	Remarks and references to Appendices
P7C88.	17	11AM	G.O.C. Division forwarded notions to officers N.C.O's & men for operations on 26.10.30 Sept. Bn. move by Motor-Lorries to TRESCAULT. Bn H.Q. Q.d.32. 57C.	
Q.d.32.	18.		Bn relieves 2/5- Notts & Derbys in the Right-Subsector of the Gouzeaucourt relief complete 7.30 P.M. Bn H.Q. K24637 57C.	N.R.S.
K24637.	19		Quiet- nothing to report.	N.R.S.
"	20		Quiet- nothing to report. 2/Lt Beckett relieved from duty.	N.R.S.
"	21		Quiet- nothing to report.	N.R.S.
"	22		Bn relieved by 2/4th. West Riding Regt. Relief completed 6.30 P.M. Bn moved to HINDENBURG LINE. Bn H.Q. R35.a. 25.25. Lt. Orchard proceeded on leave.	N.R.S.
R35a2525	23	10.30 A.M.	Bn move by march route to ROCQUIGNY arriving 2.5.0 P.M. Bn H.Q. 027 d67. 57C. 26 reinforcements reported for duty 2/Lt. Burrage reported for duty.	N.R.S.
ROCQUIGNY 027 d67	24		Bn rested. 2/Lt McGuire & 2/Lt Taylor admitted to Hospital.	N.R.S.

Cady The Sheen Wilkin R/t Lt Col.

SECRET

Army Form C. 2118.

2/4 LEICESTERSHIRE Regt.

WAR DIARY
or
INTELLIGENCE SUMMARY.

DECEMBER

(Erase heading not required.)

Place	Date	Hour	Summary of Events and Information	Remarks and references to Appendices
027d67.	25	5:30 AM	Bn moved by march route & train to LIGNEREUIL arriving at 4:30 PM. BnHQ I2/b 33. b.4/5/1 c.	ref A
LIGNEREUIL I2/b 33	26		Bn rested	ref A
"	27		Bn rested	ref A
"	28		Bn training	ref A
"	29		Bn training	ref A
"	30		36 reinforcements reported for duty. Pte Fosseu admitted to hospital sick.	ref A
"	31		Bn training. Major Barnes reported for duty.	ref A

T. Stapleton Lt Col
Cmdg 2/4 Leicestershire Regt

Original

Army Form C. 2118.

SECRET

WAR DIARY
or
INTELLIGENCE SUMMARY   2/4 LEICESTERSHIRE RGT.

JANUARY 1918.

Place	Date	Hour	Summary of Events and Information	Remarks and references to Appendices
LIGNEREUIL 12/6 3.3.	1		Bn Training	reply
B. Ln 51 a.	2		Bn Training	reply
"	3		Bn Training	reply
"	4		Bn Training 2 Lt. J.C. Bowe admitted to hospital. Capt. R.A. Henderson proceeded to Aldershot. No. attd. at S.O. Course.	reply
"	5		Bn Training	reply
"	6		Church Parade	reply
"	7		Bn Training	reply
"	8		Bn Training	reply
"	9		Bn Training	reply
"	10		Bn Training. Capt. N.S. Waite proceeded on leave	reply
"	11		Bn Training 35 Reinforcements reported for duty ex Depot Baston	reply
"	12		Bn Training	reply
"	13		Bn Sheet Parade. Distribution of gifts. Lt/Sgt. 17 total	reply
"	14		Bn Training Lt. Col. Hein Bolgarden Bt.DSO. proceeded on 30 days leave	reply
"	15		Bn Training 2/Lts. E. Roberts, N. Baylis, J.W. Abell, L. Russell reported for duty	reply

Original

SECRET

Army Form C. 2118.

WAR DIARY
INTELLIGENCE SUMMARY

2/4 LEICESTERSHIRE REGT

JANUARY

(Erase heading not required.)

Instructions regarding War Diaries and Intelligence Summaries are contained in F. S. Regs, Part II. and the Staff Manual respectively. Title Pages will be prepared in manuscript.

Place	Date	Hour	Summary of Events and Information	Remarks and references to Appendices
LIGNEROLLES	16		Bn. Training 2/Lt. Pt. Hudgell admitted to hospital	
12/6 3/3 51C	17		Bn. Training. Lt. L.B. Brigham M.C. returned from leave	
	18		Bn. Training. Lt. A.E. Thorold proceeded on leave.	
"	19		Bn. Training 2/Lt. A.T. Norby reported for duty. Bde. running contest.	
"	20		Bn. Church Parade. Prize taken by B. & E. 137 Bde.	
"	21		Bn. Training	
"	22		Bn. Training Lt. R.W.J. Short proceeded on leave. Bn. inspected by M.O.	
			Divisional	
"	23		Bn. Training 20 Reinforcements reported for duty	
"	24		Bn. Training	
"	25		Bn. Training 2/Lt. Th.S. Beckett who returned to hospital	
"	26		Bn. Training	
"	27		Church Parade.	
"	28		Bn. Training	
"	29		Bn. Training	
"	30		Bn. Training	
"	31		Bn. Training... The following Capt. reported to the unit for duty, /c— Capt. G.B. & Lt. Capt. P.W. Jones M.C. Lt. F.W. Giles, 2/Lts H.S. Miller, W.S. Miller, L.B. Sadler and 171 other ranks. J.B. Sim Major 2nd Leicestershire Regt.	

Headquarters
177th Inf Bde

1. Herewith War Diary for
the Month of February
please

1-3-18   for O.C. 2/4 Leicester Regt

ORIGINAL　　　　　　　　　　　　　　　　　　　SECRET

WAR DIARY 2/4 LEICESTER REGIMENT
INTELLIGENCE SUMMARY

Army Form C. 2118.

(Erase heading not required.)

Instructions regarding War Diaries and Intelligence Summaries are contained in F.S. Regs., Part II. and the Staff Manual respectively. Title pages will be prepared in manuscript.

Hour, Date, Place	Summary of Events and Information	Remarks and references to Appendices
1.2.18 LIGNEREUIL 51C. /21.b 3.3	Re-organization of Battalion into 4 platoons per company by absorbing draft from 2/5 LEICESTER. REGT	Appx3
2.2.18 do. do.	TRAINING.	Appx3
3.2.18 do. do.	"	Appx3
4.2.18 do. do.	"	Appx3
5.2.18 do. do.	Inspection of Brigade at AMBRINES (1 mile from billet) by Commander of VI Corps Lt.Gen. Sir AYLMER HALDANE. K.C.B. D.S.O.	Appx3
6.2.18	TRAINING	Appx3
7.2.18	"	Appx3
8.2.18	"	Appx3
9.2.18	Proceeded by march route to BAVINCOURT, starting 11.a.m arriving at destination 3.0 p.m distance 7½ miles.	G.O.3. Order No.66 attached
10.2.18 BAVINCOURT 51C. P 34.d.8.6	Proceeded by march route to BLAIREVILLE, starting 10.30.a.m arriving 3.0.p.m. distance 8 miles	J.U.O. Order No.67 attached
11.2.18 BLAIREVILLE 51C X 4.d.3.2	march route to ARMAGH CAMP. starting 10.30 reaching camp 2.0.p.m distance 5½ miles	J.U.O. Order No.68 attached

ORIGINAL

SECRET

WAR DIARY 2/4 LEICESTER REGT.

or

INTELLIGENCE SUMMARY.

Army Form C. 2118.

(Erase heading not required.)

Instructions regarding War Diaries and Intelligence Summaries are contained in F.S. Regs., Part II. and the Staff Manual respectively. Title pages will be prepared in manuscript.

Hour, Date, Place	Summary of Events and Information	Remarks and references to Appendices
12.2.18 ARMAGH CAMP 51.B. S23.c.8.4.	Left camp by motor lorry column at 3.45 p.m. and met guides. Transit 3½ miles to lorries and relieved 12th Suffolks (121st Infantry Bde) in right sub-sector of Brigade front (near BULLECOURT) relief complete 10.35 p.m.	JWB Orders No 69 attached
13.2.18 U.28.c.8.4	Quiet day. No 3 post within 30 yards of enemy.	JWB
14.2.18 U.28.c.8.4.	Quiet day. 1 direct hit on No 9 post Lewis Gun team knocked out. Sole survivor Smith recommended for M.M. Heavy shelling on Bn H.Qrs at 7.30 p.m.	JWB
15.2.18 do. do.	Barrage at 5.30 a.m. Quiet day after.	JWB
16.2.18 do. do.	Quiet day	JWB
17.2.18 do. do.	Quiet day	JWB
18.2.18	Relieved by 2/4 LINCOLN. REGT. Relief complete by 10.15 p.m. last company "D" caught in shell fire & delayed 3 hours. Went into L'ABBAYE CAMP MORY in Brigade Reserve.	JWB Orders No 71 attached
J.W. Burnett Major.
Comdg 2/4 Leicester Regt.

ORIGINAL

SECRET

WAR DIARY 2/4 LEICESTER REGT.

Army Form C. 2118.

Instructions regarding War Diaries and Intelligence Summaries are contained in F.S. Regs., Part II. and the Staff Manual respectively. Title pages will be prepared in manuscript.

INTELLIGENCE SUMMARY.

(Erase heading not required.)

Hour, Date, Place	Summary of Events and Information	Remarks and references to Appendices
19/2/18 Mony 57.c / B22.a.7.3	Day spent in cleaning up generally. 300 men on digging Fatigue Noreuil - Ecourt Line from 4.30pm - 8.15 am.	I/c
20/2/18 Do	All Companies held Kit inspection. H Q Coy test C Coy at Football 4-0. Good game. Raised during evening.	I/c
21 - - Do	Batt Parade under C.O 12 Noon. H Q Coy beat B Coy at Football 4-1. C Coy beat A Coy 2-1. Batt Concert at 6 pm at which all comps helped. Very good.	I/c
22 - - Do	Specialist Training all morning. 300 Men on digging fatigue Noreuil & Ecourt Line. 4.30pm - 7.30 am	I/c

= Petroleum
K.Coe
Comdg 2/4 Leicester Regt"

ORIGINAL

SECRET.
2/4 LEICESTER REGT. Army Form C. 2118.

WAR DIARY
or
INTELLIGENCE SUMMARY.
(Erase heading not required.)

Hour, Date, Place	Summary of Events and Information	Remarks and references to Appendices
23/2/18 MORY	Batt bathing and having Anti Tanks Foot Inspt. went all day. At 6 PM Very good show by 2/1.N.Mid F.A. Punnets Troupe for Battn.	I.C
24 ~ DO	At 6 pm Battn Paraded by Companies and marched via Ecoust and Bullecourt to the over left Sub Sector of Centre Brigade Training very quiet night Batt relief went off well. Relief completed by 10 pm. The Germans is held by a system of Posts The Germans are from 5 to 1000 yds away left to Sanotte and fa Waldgren Watts, and Ferstures went home to England on a 6 months substitution scheme "C" and "B" Companies hold the Front Line "D" in Sup/port and "C" in reserve. Battn Frontage from V22.D.0.6. - V.21.D.4.8. (Bullecourt Map)	I.C Colghan M.C06 2/4 Leicester Regt
Bullecourt		

ORIGINAL

SECRET.

WAR DIARY 2/4 LEICESTER REGT.
or
INTELLIGENCE SUMMARY.

Army Form C. 2118.

Instructions regarding War Diaries and Intelligence Summaries are contained in F. S. Regs., Part II. and the Staff Manual respectively. Title pages will be prepared in manuscript.

(Erase heading not required.)

Hour, Date, Place	Summary of Events and Information	Remarks and references to Appendices
25th Feb. Bullecourt.	Dull showery Morning. Trenches very muddy. Very quiet day. Were warned though Army that Germans intended to attack at Dawn to-morrow. At 10.15 pm Germans attempted bombing raid on the Division on our left (3rd Div.) The S.O.S. went up and heavy gun fire went on for an hour.	T.C
26/2/18/ DO.	Fine Frosty Morning and very quiet. At Noon a German Aeroplane was brought down by A.A. gun falling just outside our Lines. The Pilot came down in the Reserve Line dead. Two Patrols went out from Front Line Confirmed !!	T.C
27 " " DO	Dull Cloudy day and very quiet at Midnight very heavy gun fire from the Direction of Arras. 2 Patrols from Front line Coy.	T.C
28 " " DO	Showery Morning. Trenches very wet. Quiet day and very little shelling. Joining the Leicester Regt.	T.C Lt. Clapham. W.Bool Lt. Rear

(73989) W4141—463. 400,000. 9/14. H.&J.Ltd. Forms/C. 2118/10.

ORIGINAL
SECRET.

Army Form C. 2118.

2/4 LEICESTER REGT.

WAR DIARY
or
INTELLIGENCE SUMMARY.
(Erase heading not required.)

Instructions regarding War Diaries and Intelligence Summaries are contained in F.S. Regs., Part II. and the Staff Manual respectively. Title pages will be prepared in manuscript.

Hour, Date, Place	Summary of Events and Information	Remarks and references to Appendices
28/2/18 Bulscourt	at 7.40 P.m. after artillery and Trench Mortar preparation, ft Raby took out a strong party with the object of obtaining identification by prisoner. The Patrol went out from No 2 Post but found that the Germans had evacuated their Trench after examining Trench system the Party returned to No 2 Post. Very quiet night. U 22. c. 5.5. At 9.30 P.m.	I.C. I.C Clayhorn. Kool. Lomag 2/4 Leicester Regt.

2/4th LEICESTERSHIRE REGIMENT.　　ORDER No 68　　　　　Copy No

Ref Sheet 51.c and Lens 11　　　　　　　　　　　　　　8.2.18

    1. The 177th Infantry Brigade Group will march to the Gouy-en-Artois area tomorrow 9.2.18 and to Blaireville area on 10.2.18

    2. The Battalion will march to BAVINCOURT (distance about 7½ miles)

    3. Starting point. Cross roads immediately S.of Transport Lines.

    4. Time of starting 11.30 am. Order of march. Bn.H.Q. C.D.A.B.and Transport.

Instructions.

    5. (a) Lt.L.B.Orchard M.C. and the Coy Billeting N.C.Os will be at Brigade H.Q. at LIGNEREUIL at 8.0 am to proceed by Lorry.
       (b) Blankets and Coy Boxes will be at Q.M.Stores at 7.30 am.
       Officers Kits will be at Q.M.Stores at 10.0 am.
       Each Coy will send a N.C.O 1/c of blanket party who will be responsible that his Company blankets are loaded.
       Maltese Cart will be at R.A.P. at 9.30 am.
       Mess Cart will be at H.Q.Mess at 9.30 am.
       Dress:- F.S.M.O. Jerkins will not be worn.

       Company Mess boxes for conveyance in the Mess Cart and 1.mess man per Coy will be at Q.M.Stores at 9.45 am

                        W.R.Sowter, 2/Lth& A/Adjt.
                        2/4th Leicestershire Regt.

Issued by runner at 12.30 am.

Distribution.

    1. A.Coy
    2. B. "
    3. C. "
    4. D. "
    5. BNHQ.
    6. Quartermaster.
    7. Transport Ofcer.
    8. Billeting Officer.
    9. Officers Mess.
   10. Retained.

SECRET.   2/4th LEICESTERSHIRE REGIMENT.   Order No.67   Copy No.

Ref Sheet 51.c. and Lens 11.   9.2.18

1. The 177th Infantry Brigade Group will move to the
   BLAIREVILLE Area on the 10th.

2. The Battalion will march to No.2 Camp BLAIREVILLE
   tomorrow the 10.2.18.

3. Starting point - Road junction P36.c.3.2.
   Route - cross roads V5.b.2.2. - LE-Bac-Du-Sud - X roads
   Q 27.d.9s.5c. - BASSEUX - BELLACOURT - BRETENCOURT.
   (distance about 8 miles)
   Time of starting 11.0 am.
   Order of March.
        Bn.H.Q. D.A.B.C. and Transport.

4. 2/Lt.A.Springate and 1.billeting N.C.O. per Coy and 1
   for Bn.H.Q. will be at Brigade Headquarters at GOUY-
   EN-ARTOIS at 8.0 am.

Instructions.
5. Blankets etc will be at Q.M.Stores at 9.0 am.
   Officers Kits " " " " " " " " 9.30 am
   One Mess box per Coy. and 1.man will be at Q.M.Stores
   at 9.30 am to proceed with Mess Cart.
   Remainder of Coy Mess stores will be carried on their
   L.G.limbers.
   Dress as to-day.

                                    W.R.Sowter, 2/Lt & A/Adjt.
                                    2/4th Leicestershire Regt.

Issued by runner at 8.30 pm.

Distribution.

Copy No 1.   A.Coy.
       2.   B.Coy.
       3.   C.Coy.
       4.   D.Coy.
       5.   T.O.
       6.   Qr.Mr.
       7.   2/Lt.Springate.
       8.   Bn.H.Q.
       9.   Retained.
      10.   War Diary.

SECRET.   a/4th LEICESTERSHIRE REGIMENT. Order No.62   Copy No 10.

Reference: LENS 11
51 b S.W.
57 c N.W.
51 c

1. The 177th Infantry Brigade will march to the Reserve
   Division Area on Feb 11th, and relieve the 181st
   Infantry Brigade in the BULLECOURT Sector on the
   night 12/13 February.

2. The Battalion will proceed by march route tomorrow
   H.2.to to ADINKN CAMP (S 22 b.c.5) (51 b.S.W.)

3. Starting point:- Southern end of Camp clear of Transport
   Lines.
   Time of starting 10.5 am.
   Route:- HENDECOURT - BOIRY - ST MARTIN (distance
   about 5½ miles)
   Order of march:- Bn.H.Q.A.B.C.D. and Transport.
   An interval of 200 yds will be kept between Companies

4. Lt.L.B.Orchard.M.C. and the 5 billeting N.C.Os will
   be at Brigade Headquarters on cycles at 8.0 am.
   Report Bn.H.Q. at 7.30 am.

Instructions 5. Blankets etc. will be at Q.M.Stores at 9.0 am.
   Officers Kits "   "   "   "   "   "   9.15 am.
   Mess Cart will go with the Transport.
   One mess box per Coy will go on the Mess Cart, these
   will be at Q.M.Stores at 9.30 am.
   Remaining Coy mess stores will go on their L.G.limbers
   Dress:- As for to-day.
   7.0 am Reveille.
   8.0 am Breakfast.
   OsC Coys will ensure huts are left clean.

                            F.Waldron,2/Lt.A/Adjt.
                            a/4th Leicestershire Regt.

Issued by Runner at 6.45 pm.

Copy No 1. to A.Coy.
        2. " B. "
        3. " C. "
        4. " D. "
        5. " T.O.
        6. " Qr.Mr.
        7. " Lt.L.B.Orchard.M.C.
        8. " Bn.H.Q.
        9. " Retained.
       10. " War Diary.

SECRET.

2/4th LEICESTERSHIRE REGIMENT. Order No. ??   Copy No. 9.

Reference: sheet 57c N.W.

1. The 177th Inf.Div. will relieve the 181st Inf.Bde. to-night 19/15th

2. The Battalion will relieve the 12th Suffolks

3. Details of relief.
   A.Coy   Right front line.
   B.Coy   Left front line.
   C.Coy   Support Company.
   D.Coy   Reserve Company.

   Guides as detailed will be at X roads B 24.d.7.8.
   (sugar factory) at 6.30 pm.
   Bn.H.Q.   1 guide
   A.Coy   1 "   Posts 1 & 2 and London.
               1 "   "   3
               1 "   "   12 S (Tank Post) and
                                Joy Ride Block.
               1 "   "   13 S (Tank Avenue)
               1 "   Coy H.Q.
   B.Coy   1 "   Post 4
               1 "   "   5 & 6
               1 "   "   10 S (Joy Ride post)
               1 "   "   11 S
               1 "   Coy H.Q.
   C.Coy   1 "   per Platoon
               1 "   Post 8
               1 "   "   9 S
   D.Coy   1 "   per Platoon

   All guides will have a ticket showing Unit whom they are guiding and their posts.
   Duplicate tickets issued to Coy Commanders.

   Lewis Guns, Stretchers, and Signalling kit to be carried

   Route to be taken by relieving Coys.
   BULLECOURT AVENUE - RAILWAY RESERVE N-DUCKBOARDS

Instructions 4. The Battalion will be on Football ground EAST of present camp at 3.10 pm formed in parties in the order detailed for relief.

   Parties will be ready to "embus" at this time in this order

   Rations for 15th to be taken on the men.

   Dress: F.S.M.O. (steel helmets, jerkins worn, box respirators at the alert)

   Officers trench bundles and Coy Mess boxes, dixies, canteen stores, hot food containers to be stacked in Coy dumps in front of Orderly Room by 12 noon.

   All ranks not proceeding to the line will report to Q.M.Stores by 3.15 pm.

   Blankets to be at Q.M.Stores by 12 noon
   Officers kits to be at Q.M.Stores by 12 noon.

   Transport will not pass X roads B 24.d.7.8. before 7.0 pm.

   Transport Officer will leave D.Coys kit at their H.Qrs and deliver the remainder of stores to Bn.H.Q.

O.C. A Coy. will see that all men in Battle Dress burn
their scraps of craft in the Bin.

2. Kits for Baggage Car will be outside the Billet
at 7-30.

3. Reveille Parties complete 05 Case Rds & Ammo.

F. Stapleton Lt. MGC
2/5th Lancashire Regt.

Issued by runner at 7.45 pm

Coys No 1. "A" Coy Annes
"   2. "   "   Balby
"   3. "   "   Catley
"   4. "   "   Brown
"   5. "   "   Clark
"   6. "   "   Mills
"   7. "   "   Shields
"   8. "   "   Robinson
"   9. "   "   Van Praag

SECRET.   4/4th LEICESTERSHIRE REGIMENT. Order No. ?.   Copy No. 10

REF: 57 c N.W.

1. The 4th Lincolns will relieve the 4th Leicesters in
   the right sub-sector on the night 15/16 th February
   The 4th Leicesters will go into Reserve at L'Abbaye
   Camp KOMX.
2. Details of relief.
   Guides as detailed under 2/Lt.Springate, I.M. will meet
   4th Lincolns at junction of track and road at S.8.c.10.4.
   at 5.0 pm (instructions issued separately.)
   Tables of guides, relief, and order of going up.

   4th Leicesters.   4th Lincolns.
   C.Coy. 1 guide for Post 1   D.Coy.
     "   1   "   "   "   S.O.T.
     "   1   "   "   "   2a
     "   1   "   "   "   3
     "   1   "   "   "   4
     "   1   "   "   "   Coy.H.Q.
   D.Coy. 1   "   "   "   Post R.F.London   C.A.Coy.
     "   1   "   "   "   11
     "   1   "   "   "   12
     "   1   "   "   "   14
     "   1   "   "   "   Coy.H.Q.
   B.Coy. 1   "   "   "   each platoon   C.Coy.
                              C.H.Q. with 1 platoon
   A.Coy. 1   "   "   "   each platoon   B.Coy.
                              C.H.Q. with 1 platoon
   Bn.H.Q. 1   "   Bn.H.Q.

   Company Commanders will see that their guides each have
   a ticket showing relieving Unit when they are guiding
   and their posts.
   Route to be taken.
   Incoming Unit. MILLENARY AVENUE-GULLEY RESERVE-
   DUCKBOARDS overland.
   Outgoing Unit. TANK AVENUE-RAILWAY RESERVE-BULLECOURT
   AVENUE-overland track-road to B.4.d.7.?.-road to
   KOMX.
   Lewis Gun drums, 2 dixies per Company and all petrol
   tins and trench stores to be handed over and receipts
   taken.
   Platoons will move off complete when relieved.
   O.C.Coys will see that no stray men are wandering about
   but all come down in formed parties.

Instructions 3. C.D.& B.Coys Officers kits, mess stores, spare dixies,
   food containers, will be stacked outside Bn.H.Q. by
   7.0pm.in Company dumps with 2 men per Company in
   charge.
   4. 2 limbers will report at intervals to Bn.H.Q. for
   these.
   1.whole limber will report to A.Coy (Reserve) for BB
   blankets and stores.
   A.whole limber will be at X roads B.4.d.7.8. and
   remain there until the last platoon has passed. This
   limber is for Lewis guns and signalling kit.
   All platoons and limbers will report at gateway
   entrance,L'Abbaye Camp pass along individually.
   Capt Blunt and 2 O.c.B.Coys, R.S.M., I/c Bn.Sgts.
   will report to Major J.C.Snaith at L'Abbaye Camp at
   9.30 pm.
   The Transport Officer will arrange for Officers Kits,
   Mess stores,mens blankets etc. from Transport Lines
   to be at L'Abbaye Camp by 8.0 pm with all details to
   rejoin Companies.
   The Quartermaster will arrange for the cookers to be
   at L'Abbaye Camp by 7.0 pm.
   Tea and a meal will be kept ready.

4. Report relief complete by code "SUNSHINE" to Bn.H.Q. by line and personally at HQRY.

5. ACKNOWLEDGE.

                                   P.Waldron, 2/Lt & A/Adjt
                            2/5th Leicestershire Regt.

Issued by runner at 8.30 pm.

Copy No. 1. to 177th Inf.Bde.
        2. " 4th Lincolns.
        3. " A.Coy.
        4. " B "
        5. " C "
        6. " D "
        7. " T.O & Q.M.
        8. " 2/Lt Springate, E.M.
        9. " Bn.H.Q.
      10. " Retained.
      11. " War Diary.

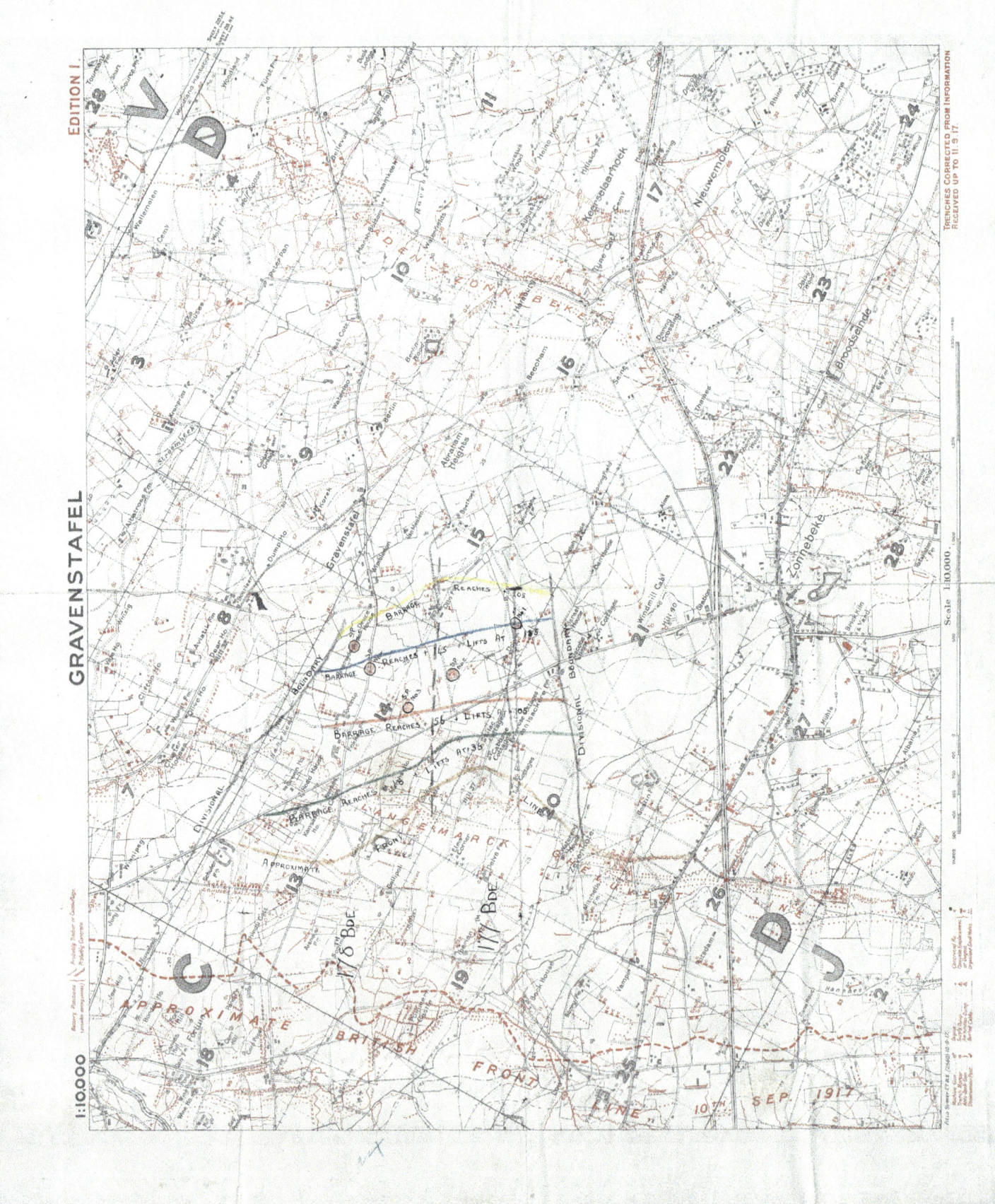

59th Division.
177th Infantry Brigade.

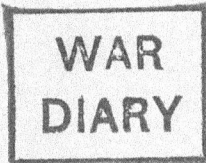
WAR DIARY

2/4th BATTALION

THE LECEISTERSHIRE REGIMENT

MARCH 1918

Attached :- Report on Operations commencing 21st.

ORIGINAL

2/4 LEICESTER REGT

Army Form C. 2118.

WAR DIARY
or
INTELLIGENCE SUMMARY.
(Erase heading not required.)

Instructions regarding War Diaries and Intelligence Summaries are contained in F.S. Regs., Part II. and the Staff Manual respectively. Title pages will be prepared in manuscript.

Hour	Date, Place	Summary of Events and Information	Remarks and references to Appendices
	March 1. 1918. BULLECOURT	Quiet day - foggy.	
	" 2 "	Cold & misty. Quiet day. Inter-company relief.	
	" 3 "	Snow fell. Raid in German lines. Tractor moving	
	" 4 "	American Officer attached. (Small raid carried out by Capt Oliver + Lt. Orchard.	
	" 5 "	Quiet day	
	" 6 "	Raid on our right. Retaliation on our frontline. Corps Commander came round lines	
	" 7 "	Area shelled during night	
	" 8 "	Relieved in line by 4 Lincoln Regt. went into support of ECOUST. Quiet relief	
	" 9 "	Lovely fine day	
	" 10 "	do	
	" 11 "	do	
	" 12 "	do	
	" 13 "	Stood at 5.45 in anticipation of attack.	
	" 14 "	went into right sub-sector relieving 5 Lincoln Regt	
	" 15 "	Quiet day	
	" 16 "	do	
	" 17 "	do	
	" 18 "	800 drums of gas fired into German lines.	
	" 19 "	Raid at 8.0 pm by 2/Lt BERRIDGE + 8 O.R. One German captured. 3 killed. No casualties to us. Returned at night. Raid at 8.0 pm by 2/Lt. S. Stafford Regt.	

(73989) W4141—463. 400,000. 9/14. H.&J.Ltd. Forms/C. 2118/10.

SECRET · ORIGINAL
Army Form C. 2118.

2/4 LEICESTER REGT

WAR DIARY or INTELLIGENCE SUMMARY

(Erase heading not required.)

Place	Date	Hour	Summary of Events and Information	Remarks and references to Appendices
MORY	20.		in Divisional Reserve. Stood to at 4:45 a.m. to 7:30 a.m.	F.c.
"	21	5.0 am	At 5 a.m. message received from Brigade to "Stand to"; very heavy artillery fire all round. SAA bombs. SAA flares were issued.	F.c.
		6.0 am	moved to point of assembly at B.17.d.	
		6.0 am – 12 noon	Stayed at assembly point. Misty morning. All wires cut to front line, no runs available at 10 a.m. the silent guns opened fir S.O.S.	
		12 noon	ordered to take up position in support line 2nd system. moved up in artillery formation and avoided German Barrage. A Coy leading before reaching objective came under heavy M.G. fire, and saw several discoloured Germans advancing from ECOUST. A Coy extended and carried remainder of Battalion with it taking up a position in front line 3rd system. Battalion in position in touch on right with Lincolns, but left flank in the air. Line only spitlocked & men deep in.	
		2.30 pm	Germans seen in masses 800 yards away & gradually working closer.	
		4 pm	Hostile attack in strength developed along HOGS BACK on our left.	
		5 pm	Konferenmen filled gap. Germans seemed to advance. Battalion suffered about 30 casualties. Lt. ORSON killed, 2/Lt BERRIDGE & ORCHARD wounded. Artillery fire was not heavy all day. Capt. WILLIAMS Patrol captured a German R.A.M.C. officer + 4 men.	2/Lt. Archer, 2/Lt. Lowe, 2/Lt. Webster killed

SECRET • ORIGINAL 2/4

Army Form C. 2118.

WAR DIARY
or
INTELLIGENCE SUMMARY
LEICESTER REGT

(Erase heading not required.)

Instructions regarding War Diaries and Intelligence Summaries are contained in F.S. Regs., Part II. and the Staff Manual respectively. Title Pages will be prepared in manuscript.

Place	Date	Hour	Summary of Events and Information	Remarks and references to Appendices
MORY	21st		The battalion having been in the line 2½ days continuously during that time, all ranks were tired and badly in need of sleep. Night quiet & very cold.	I.C
"	22nd	5.30 a.m.	19/17th H.L.I. relieved Battalion, who took up a new position in outpost line B.3 system. B.17.B. 3.4 B.24.A 3.6	I.C
		8.30 a.m.	In position, line running between VRAUCOURT and ST LEGER. Intense aeroplane activity, but little shelling.
		4.0 p.m.	German attack developed on front line, but F.6 ECOUST - VRAUCOURT Rd and a small section of trench was lost.
		5.30 p.m.	Right flank on neat Divisional front withdrew, having orders to form a new line S.W. of VRAUCOURT. The troops on our right conformed to this movement & the Battalion also withdrew to the Army line in front of MORY.
		6.30 p.m.	In position and men digging in. German levy in VRAUCOURT, an attack developed on both our flanks simultaneously. Several advanced posts were killed or captured about this hostile attack was held up. Lt HUTCHINSON & BECKETT & about 30 men were brought in missing. The Germans worked through a gap on our left and attempted to cut the Battalion off by getting between it and MORY.

Lt Col ----
Comdg 2/4 Leicest. Regt

2449 Wt. W14957/M90 750,000 1/16 J.B.C. & A. Forms/C.2118/12.

SECRET ORIGINAL

Army Form C. 2118.

2/4. LEICESTER REGT

WAR DIARY
or
INTELLIGENCE SUMMARY

(Erase heading not required.)

Place	Date	Hour	Summary of Events and Information	Remarks and references to Appendices
MORY	22nd	3.30 pm	Got On information situation to Brigade through telephone received orders to withdraw to a new position defending MORY as far as possible	T.C
		4.0 pm	Battalion formed up in close order rendezvous in column of route down MORY Rd with flank Guard. B/personnel captured in route.	
		10.0 pm	Battalion took up a position in MORY astride the main road with outposts covering the main position which was held in posts. In touch north & knuckles on right and elements of Suffolk & Middlesex Regts on our left.	
"	23rd	11.30 – 4 am	At 11.15 pm a hostile attack drove in the outpost line and turned our Left Flank by forcing back The Suffolk Regiment. From continuous attacks on The Batt from Front and Left Flank all of which were held up by rapid fire. The Germans continually reformed and attacked. Blowing Trumpets and cheering but failed to penetrate out line. Their casualties must have been very heavy. They brought up a light Trench Mortar and a high Velocity gun and inflicted casualties with these	I.C
		4 am – 5 am	Firing died down and attacks ceased	
		6 am	Batt withdrew by Companies to High Ground E. of Ervillers and dug in there. 3 Companies in firing line and one in support. Ervillers & Behag...	

WAR DIARY or INTELLIGENCE SUMMARY

ORIGINAL Army Form C. 2118.

2/4 LEICESTER. REGT

Place	Date	Hour	Summary of Events and Information	Remarks and references to Appendices
ERVILLERS	23rd	6.30 a.m.	Slight shelling.	I.C.
		7.30 a.m.	Germans showed no intention to advance, but could be seen moving about on High Ground N. of MORY.	
			East Sentry. (Ronen Batt.) & Middlesex Regt. both 40th Division counter attacked high ground between MORY and ST. LEGER. But much little progress on right.	I.C.
			Remainder of day quiet	
		10.0 p.m.	Bombed by aeroplanes	
	24th		Quiet day.	
		3-4 p.m.	ERVILLERS. shelled.	
		6.30 p.m.	relief orders came in.	
		9.0 p.m.	Bombing & shelling started	
		10.0 p.m.	Hostile attack developed on our left facing trench SUFFOLKS & MIDDLESEX Regts. Germans broke through & lined MORY-ERVILLERS RD. enfilading the whole of our line. Bon Myr. formed up facing road & A Coy counter attacked Germans. M.G. fire too heavy. Eleven? A Coy could muster little progress owing to heavy casualties. They eventually formed a line facing MORY-ERVILLERS. Rd. held the Germans attack up from that. teaming. Their attack got Hill & 2 men rushed a German M.G. Gun billets an Offrs & 7 opened up [illegible] Lieut [illegible] Hopes. Curtis [illegible]	

ORIGINAL
1/4 LEICESTER REGT.

SECRET

Army Form C. 2118.

WAR DIARY
INTELLIGENCE SUMMARY

(Erase heading not required.)

Instructions regarding War Diaries and Intelligence Summaries are contained in F. S. Regs., Part II. and the Staff Manual respectively. Title Pages will be prepared in manuscript.

Place	Date	Hour	Summary of Events and Information	Remarks and references to Appendices
ERVILLERS	24th	11.30 p.m.	A Coy held the line, but all attempts even to maintain touch or of S.A.A. failed owing to very heavy M.G. fire.	III C
"		12.0 p.m.		
"	25th	1.0 a.m.	One Coy of the WELSH REGT. attempted to reinforce them, but found it impossible and suffered many casualties.	III C
		1.0 – 4.30 a.m.	Heavy M.G. fire and any movement was impossible owing to the bright moonlight.	
		4.30 – 5.30 a.m.	Enemy died down and a few of our casualties were cleared.	
		7.30 a.m.	After very heavy M.G. fire Germans rushed the line from left flank in large numbers, and all the posts, all of which resisted to the last were either killed or captured. A few men from each company fighting their way back to the ERVILLERS—BEHAGNIES Rd. The battalion consisted of C.O. +25 men.	
		10.30 a.m.	Remaining men took a position in support of the LINCOLNS, relieving the roads. BEHAGNIES was evacuated by the division on our right and conforming the movement of the LINCOLNS we fell back to a new line covering GOMIECOURT.	
		1.30 p.m.		
		2.30 / 3.0 p.m.	And the Germans could be seen in large numbers coming down the MORY slopes.	
		7.30 p.m.	Battalion relieved by Not Brigade. Estimated casualties 16 officers, known 1 of OC and 414 other ranks.	

Lt. A.G. /4 Leicester Regt.
Comdg /4 Leicester Regt.

SECRET.   ORIGINAL

WAR DIARY
or
INTELLIGENCE SUMMARY — 2/4 LEICESTER REGT.

Army Form C. 2118.

(Erase heading not required.)

Place	Date	Hour	Summary of Events and Information	Remarks and references to Appendices
	25th		Battalion rested at DOUCHY-LES-AYETTES.	I.C
D. les AYETTES	26th	8 a.m.	Marched via QUESNOY FARM. – GOMMECOURT – to FONQUEVILLERS when Brigade was	I.C
		2.0	concentrated by a demonstration holding the line, to form a defensive flank in OHLAHS	
		6.30 p.m.	was reported in HEBUTERNE. Marched back, billets at BIENVILLERS.	
BIENVILLERS	27th		Marched at 8 a.m. via POMMIERS – COURLEMONT. WAHLUZEL to SUS - ST. LEGER.	I.C
SUS-ST-LEGER	28th		Remained at SUS. ST. LEGER.	I.C
"	29th		Left SUS. ST LEGER at 6.30 p.m. to FREVENT and entrained there at 11 p.m. arrived HOUDAIN 2.30 a.m. marched to BEUGIN arriving 3.45 a.m.	I.C
HOUDAIN	30th		billetted there. men slept most of the day	I.C
BEUGIN	31st		Inspected at HOUDAIN by G.O.C. 59 U Division. Transport left at 11 a.m. for PROVEN.	I.C

A Coe
Comdg 2/4 Leicestershire Regt

21-3-18

At 5 am an order was received from Brigade to 'Stand To'. Battalion paraded and at 6 am was ordered to march to Point of Assembly.

Batt arrived at point of Assembly at 6.45 am just S.W. of VRAUCOURT ST LEGER Rd. B.17.d Central got into Artillery formation and awaited orders. Teas were issued and Patrols sent out to Front and Flanks to get in touch with situation. The shelling was very heavy all round and some Heavy Batteries near us were put out of action. The Batt sustained no casualties as the Assembly Point had been cleverly chosen. At 10 am a Gunner Officer informed us that the S.O.S had gone up from in front of Ecoust.

At 12 Noon Batt acting under orders received from Brigade at 11.40 am marched off to occupy

Support Line 2nd System just S.W. of Ecoust.
Batt started by Companies in Artillery formation and by choosing broad country Route escaped hostile barrage. A Coy were leading and were within 400 yds of their objective about C.7.d when they came under heavy Rifle and MG fire from close range suffering casualties. 2/Lt Orson was killed and Lt Orchard, 2/Lt Berridge and about 30 O.R. were wounded.
A Coy under orders from Capt Silver at once extended and opened fire. The C.O went forward to get in touch with the situation and saw several thousand Germans about 500 yds away advancing from Ecoust and along Hogs Backs Spur and.
It was obvious that the 2 Brigades in front had been cut off and the Germans were right through the Support Line of the Battle System. The C.O ordered Major Barnes to take up position in Firing Line 3rd System

with B C and D Coys whilst A
Coy covered the movement from
its present position
    At 2.30 pm A Coy also
withdrew to this line having covered
the blowing up of a Battery of
Field Guns and inflicted casualties
on the Enemy by close range fire
    The Batt/ is now in line
in the Firing line. 3rd System
from C.13.7.c to B.12.c
    Bn HQ and R.A.P at
C.13.C.2.5. We are in
touch on the right with 4th Lincolns
but our left is entirely in the
air.
    The Germans can be seen
in masses 600 yds away and
are gradually working closer
    At 3 pm a hostile attack
developed along HOGS BACK spur
but although attempted three times
was driven back by M G and rifle
fire. Shelling had completely
died down but MG fire was still
very heavy from the direction
of ECOUST.
    At 5 pm reinforcements
consisting of Transport Details

Band, Labour Men, etc came up on our left arriving most opportunely as the Germans were attempting to an advance on that Flank.

At 8pm the C.O. met Colonel Roffey 5th Lincolns and Colonel Cool 4th Lincolns and discussed the situation with them.

From 9-11pm the night was very quiet but German patrols were active.

At 11.15pm Capt Williams and 3 men captured a German R.A.M.C. Officer and 4 men on the ECOUST - VRAUCOURT Rd

The men are very tired as work during the last 2-3 weeks has been of an exceptionally heavy nature and the frequent "Stand To's" have permitted of little sleep.

22-3-18

The night passes quietly. Orders arrived that the 10/11th H.L.I. would relieve us in our present line and that we should go a few hundred yards in rear

to the support line 3rd system.
The relief was long in coming, but by
5.30 a.m it arrived and we took up our
new line running in front of the
VRAUCOURT - ST. LEGER Rd. from B.24.b.5.8
to B.7.6.4.4. Bn Hqrs & R.A.P are in a
dug out at B.18.C.1.2 with a Machine
Gun detachment of 5 guns.
We are in touch with the 5th Lincolns on
our right and the 12th Suffolks on our left.

From 9 a.m until 3 p.m the day
was quiet, little shelling or machine
gun fire. The day was hot and
visibility very good. There was intense
aeroplane activity, at least 40
hostile planes being over our lines at
the same time.

The Germans showed no great inclination
to advance, but could be seen in
small parties moving apparently
aimlessly about on the ridge S of ECOUST
& on the HOGS BACK.

About 4 p.m after preliminary machine
gun fire the German attack developed
along the ECOUST-VRAUCOURT Rd. and
down the slopes to the HIRONDELLE VALLEY.
The 120th Bde (the H.L.I & A.I.S.H) lost a
small portion of trench and lined
the road.

About 4.30 p.m the 6th Division on

our right withdrew to _____ having
had orders to form a defensive flank
facing VRAUCOURT.
This action left the right of the 177th Bde
held by the 4th & 5th Lincolns in the air.
At 6.p.m the German Very lights were
noticed to be showing round our
right and the two regiments on
our right the Lincolns were seen
withdrawing
This Battalion had no orders so remained
in position.
A message from 4th Lincolns was
received on the right of our
Battalion at 6.10 p.m as follows.
" I am moving my Battalion back to
Army line, as all the troops on my right
have withdrawn. Brigade informed "
6.10 p.m.
Being entirely isolated at 6.30 p.m
we started withdrawing by companies
from the right to the Army line
covering MORY. The Suffolks on our left
being notified of our action
Two machine guns at Bn Hqrs
gallantly covered this withdrawal.
During this movement there was
heavy machine gun fire and light
shelling on the left. Casualties
being caused.

The disposition of the Battalion in this new line was D Coy on the left in the only portion which had been dug C, B & A Coys extending the line to the right along a 4 foot bank about 150 yds in rear of the wire, with outposts in front. Arrangements were being made to dig in on the spitlocked line.

Our line was from B23.d.6.8 to B.17.c.9.5 with Bn Hqrs at Road junction at B.23.a.7.6 Machine gun fire was incessant but there was no shelling

We were in touch with 5 Division on our right, but could not gain touch on our left.

At 7.p.m attack developed on the Bn in front & on the left. The frontal attack was held up, but owing to the darkness the Germans were able to work through the gap on our left and reached the ST. LEGER – MORY Rd firing into our line from behind. 2/Lt Beebee & Lt J.C. Hutchinson were killed and about 30 O.R. casualties

During this operation Major Bunin, not being able to find the C.O got into touch with Brigade through luckily tapping a wire, and informed them he proposed to withdraw fighting on to MORY. The 4 & 5 Divisions being informed.

At this moment the C.O came in, having been out to investigate the same matter, the gap on our left. He came into contact with the Germans killing 3 & being slightly wounded himself.

The C.O agreed with the decision taken and the Battalion was collected and formed up in close order at Bn Hqrs. The German scouts 4 in number being captured at this spot during the forming up.

The Battalion withdrew in fours across country to the MORY cross roads having a small rear guard & a flank guard moving along the road.

A position was eventually selected in MORY from B.21.d.3.0 — B.21.b.8.3 — B.21.b.2.8 with one company on outpost along cross roads roads East of main position.

We immediately got in touch with elements of Suffolks, Middlesex & Essex Regts. wide on our left, but failed to establish contact with the Honolus on our right.

Various elements of various regts were collected & incorporated in our line.

Capt Jamie 177th Infantry Bde Staff now came up to inform us that the 4th Honolus were moving up in line with us on the right & that the Suffolks were holding MORY COPSE on our left.

The outposts of the Essex Regt on our left were driven in by heavy hostile attack and our outpost line withdrew to the main line of resistance.

After this, heavy hostile attack developed from the front & left. The Battalion its left being in the air once more had left flank drawn back almost parallel with the MORY-ERVILLERS Rd. The Germans were continually feeling for this flank, but we were dealing with it.

The Germans during the night constantly reformed and charged, blowing trumpets and cheering, being met each time with heavy rifle fire. They were unable to make any headway. The attack being entirely on our left & centre. The Germans eventually brought up a light trench mortar and a small

field gun and inflicted casualties we
threw. Our casualties were light, but
the hostile ones must have been very
heavy.

23.3.18

At 3.30am Capt Oliver came up from
~~Brigade~~ and went back with a report
on the situation.
We were now in touch on our right
with 4 howitzers whose line was
slightly in advance of ours, but
out of touch again on the left.

At 4.45 am 2/Lt Souter arrived and
brought orders from the 177th Brigade
that if it was considered impossible
to hold MORY, the Bn was to withdraw
to high ground in B.20, covering
ERVILLERS.
The C.O considered the present line
untenable, as the men were not
properly dug in and the Germans
by daylight would turn the left
flank as they held all the high
ground, thus enfilading our line.
This withdrawal was successfully
carried out at 5.30 a.m. the Bn the

moving by companies down the MORY
-ERVILLERS Rd, without interference
from the enemy.
A new line was taken up & dug on the
high ground East of ERVILLERS from B.20.c
— B.20.b., it being held in small
posts with 3 Companys + one in support.
The left post was on the ERVILLERS -
MORY Rd. where we joined the Suffolk Regt
who continued the line. On our right
were the 5 Lincolns.
About 7.30 am there was slight light
shelling of our position.
The remainder of the day was hot & very
quiet, with only occasional bursts
of Machine Gun fire.
The Germans can be seen in small parties
on the MORY Ridge, but they make
no attempt to advance.
During the day the Middlesex Regt
on our left assisted by the East Surrey
Pioneer Regt attempted some isolated
Company attacks to regain the high
ground near MORY, but were held up
by Machine Gun fire.
The day was sunny & warm and the
men were able to get a little sleep
of which they were badly in need.
Aeroplanes attempted to bomb our

lines at 10 p.m but did no damage.
ERVILLERS was also bombed and
casualties were caused there.
During the day the Brigadier General
came up to look at the situation.

24.3.18

Quiet and sunny day and the men
rested. ERVILLERS was shelled at
times. Small parties of Germans were
seen on MORY RIDGE reconnoitring our
lines.
During the afternoon JUDAS FARM was
very heavily shelled, and a barrage
was put down between VRAUCOURT
and BEHAGNIES. It was thought probable
that an attack was imminent.
Orders were received that afternoon
for a relief at night.
At 10.p.m as the men were getting
ready for relief, heavy rifle and
machine gun fire broke out on
our left flank. The Germans
had broken through the
Middlesex + Suffolks on our left
and the remnants of these battalions
withdrew to the ERVILLERS LINE.
This left our left flank completely
open, and the Germans at once

took advantage of this and lined the MORY-ERVILLERS Rd., thus enfilading the whole of our line.

Bn Hqrs formed to a flank in the open & by rapid fire held off the enemy. A Coy in support were ordered to counter attack. They formed up parallel to the MORY-ERVILLERS Rd and charged.

They were met by terrific machine gun fire and a lot of men fell. They continued to advance in short rushes to about 50 yds short of the road where they were completely held up.

Remnants of the Company formed a line at this point.

Lt Springate was killed, Lt Batson & Raleigh wounded and about 50 or 60 OR casualties.

Cpl Hill + 2 men attacked a wooden hut from which a hostile Machine Gun was firing bayonetting the team & smashing the gun.

From this time until 4 a.m machine gun & rifle fire from the Germans was terrific & it was impossible to evacuate the casualties

M. Below and all H.Q. men were wounded. Leaving C.O and R.S.M Smith

25. 3. 18

At 5 am the firing died down and a few of the casualties were evacuated. At 5.30 am The C.O went down to 5th Lincoln Hd qrs having been previously informed by Brigade that 2 Batts of the 7 Brigade intended to counter attack. The C.O was ordered by 177 Bde to get in touch with these Batts and give them the situation. This He attempted to do but could only find an officer and 20 men of the Regiment who had no orders

At 7 am The Enemy after Heavy rifle and M G fire from the left Flank formed up in the MORY- ERVILLERS Rd in large numbers and attacked along our whole line. As the attack came from enfilade many of the men were unable to fire but the Posts resisted to the ust. About 80 men fought their way back, the remainder of the Battalion being either killed or taken prisoner.

The C.O. who was in Croiller at the Time endeavouring to get in Touch with the Counter Attack Battalions returned at this moment and collecting the remnants of the Batt put them in support of 5th Lincolns.

At 10 a.m. Major Baines brought up 60 men from Transport Lines and reached GOMMIECOURT at Bde Hqrs & then went on to 5 Lincoln Hqrs. On learning the situation he formed a defensive flank facing BEHAGNIES. This position was held until relieved at night by 42nd Division.

The remnants of the Battalion marched to ~~DOUCY~~ BUCQUOY and billeted there.

T.. Colquhoun
Lt Col
Commanding
2/4 Batt^n Linc. Regt

177th Brigade.
59th Division.

2/4th BATTALION

LEICESTERSHIRE REGIMENT

APRIL 1918. /May 1918.

ORIGINAL

SECRET
Army Form C. 2118.

WAR DIARY 2/4 LEICESTER REGT.
or
INTELLIGENCE SUMMARY.
(Erase heading not required.)

Place	Date	Hour	Summary of Events and Information	Remarks and references to Appendices
BEUGIN.	1.4.18		Battalion moved by train 2.0 p.m. to PROVEN thence by march route to	
L.3.b. Sheet 27.	2.4.18		SCHOOL CAMP WATOU Ref L.3.b. Sheet 27.	
do	3.4.18		Reorganization 20 Reinforcements reported	
			" C.O and Company Officers visited new line, in	
			front of ZONNEBEKE. Brigade inspection by Army Commander.	
do	4.4.18		H.Q. Reinforcement reported ex Base. Battalion moved by light	
			Railway from POPERINGHE to POTIJZE. thence by march route to	
			ST JEAN. CAMP. I.3.b.3 & Sheet 28.	
ST JEAN CAMP I.3.b.3 &	5.4.18		All Officers and Platoon Sergeants visited the line	
do	6.4.18		Battalion Training	
do	7.4.18		" " 66 Reinforcements reported for duty ex Base	
do	8.4.18		" "	
do	9.4.18		" "	
do	10.4.18		Battalion "STOOD TO" & occupied Divisional line at dawn. C&D Coys	
			returned to ST JEAN CAMP at 9.15 am.	

ORIGINAL

SECRET.
Army Form C. 2118.

WAR DIARY 2/4. LEICESTER REGT.
INTELLIGENCE SUMMARY
(Erase heading not required.)

Place	Date	Hour	Summary of Events and Information	Remarks and references to Appendices
ST JEAN CAMP I.5.6.3.4.16.4.18			Battalion relieved 2/5th LINCOLN REGT in Left Sub Sector C+D. HQ taken up by lorry at 5.30pm. Relief Complete by 9.0pm. Bn HQ ZONNEBEKE D21d 9.2	T.C
ZONNEBEKE D21.d.9.2	11.4.18		Quiet day.	T.C
do.	12.4.18		Battalion relieved by 18th K.R.R. Relief Complete 2.0 am 13/4/18 Marched to BORRI FARM thence by Light Railway to BRANDHOEK. Battalion marches to St Lawrence Camp	T.C
ST LAWRENCE CAMP BRANDHOEK	13.4.18		Battalion moved by train from BRANDHOEK STN. at 4.0pm arrived GODNEARSVELDE at 5.0pm. Battalion Marches to BERTHEM and billets. three 2/Lt CH GROSS + 66 other rank Reinforcements arrive.	T.C
BERTHEM	14.4.18		Battalion paraded 5.0 am and Marched to LOCRE and billets in Hut. Battalion moved to Sunken Road S5a Sheet 28 in Support	T.C
S5a Sheet 28	15.4.18		2.30 am Battalion stood to in field South of road. Germans attacked about 3.0pm all appendix attached	T.C
do	16.4.18		12.30 am Battalion withdrew to SOUTHALL Camp South of LOCRE. 5.30pm Battalion moved up in artillery formation into Assembly position M29.a.4.8. withdrew back to camp at 11.0pm 15 O/r's from 7th Welch Regt	T.C

ORIGINAL SECRET.
Army Form C. 2118.

WAR DIARY 1/4 LEICESTER REGT.
or
INTELLIGENCE SUMMARY.
(Erase heading not required.)

Place	Date	Hour	Summary of Events and Information	Remarks and references to Appendices
SOUTH HILL CAMP M.17.d.0.0	17.4.18		Battalion returned to assembly position 9.0am Heavily shelled. casualties approx 80 including a few gassed. Withdrew at 10.30pm	T.C.
to WINDMILL CAMP				
WINDMILL CAMP	18.4.18		Battalion moved off to assembly position. 8.0pm A Coy attached to 2nd Sherwoods. D Coy to 1 Leicesters in support in RED LINE	T.C.
M.29.a.4.8	19.4.18		Battalion relieved by French troops 6th Coy 85th Regt Battalion. withdrew to RENINGHELST. arriving between 3.0 am + 4.0 am	T.C.
RENINGHELST.	20.4.18		Battalion marched to DIRTY BUCKET CAMP near VLAMERTINGHE arriving 5.0pm	T.C.
DIRTY BUCKET CAMP VLAMERTINGHE	21.4.18		Battalion marched at 9.15 am to billets near HOUTKERQUE arriving 1.0pm	T.C.
E.7.c.3.1.	22.4.18		Bn. HQ E.7.c.3.1. Reorganisation and training	
do	23.4.18		Training 2/Lt Hill and 2/Lt Fox and 32 other rank reinforcements arrived.	T.C.
do	24.4.18		Training	T.C.
do	25.4.18		Training	T.C.

Cleghorn Col
Comdg 1/4 Leicester Regt

ORIGINAL

SECRET
2/4 LEICESTER REGT.
Army Form C. 2118.

WAR DIARY
or
INTELLIGENCE SUMMARY

(Erase heading not required.)

Place	Date	Hour	Summary of Events and Information	Remarks and references to Appendices
E.9.C.31.	26.4.18		Battalion paraded for digging trenches near HERZEELE. Battalion returned at once and were ordered to move to SCHOOL CAMP.	E.C.
SCHOOL CAMP WATOU	27.4.18		WATOU. Battalion taken up by lorry. Battalion moved at 6.30 p.m. to trenches S. of POPERINGHE. Battalion relieves the 15th Royal Scots. Relief complete 12.30 a.m. Battalion situated in East POPERINGHE LINE. Battn HQ G.25.d.6.9	E.C.
G.25.d.6.9	28.4.18		"D" Coy took over part of 5th LINCOLN LINE on the right. Germans attacks from DICKEBUSH to LOCRE. Attack failed.	E.C.
do.	29.4.18		Quiet day	E.C.
do.	30.4.18		" " Both artillery active on our Right. Trenches improved and wired	E.C.

= Coleghoff Col
Comdg 2/4 Leicester Regt.

2/4th Bn Leicestershire Regt

Summary of Operations 14th to 18th April 1918

14th. Bn ordered to move into Support position along Sunken Road, in S.5.a & b. (running East & West)

15th Bn "Stood to" ready to move in fields South of road before mentioned about 2.30 p.m.

About 3.45 p.m. 'C' Coy, was ordered to proceed to 4th Lincolns and occupy high ground about S.17 central as a garrison for that locality. This Coy was unable to reach their destination as the enemy had occupied the crest of the RAVELSBERG RIDGE. - The Coy, deployed along road in S.10.d. & S.11.a. and advanced to a line running from S.17.a.1.9. to S.11.b.4.3. filling a gap in what appeared to be the front line, as no British troops could be seen in front of them. The Coy was then in touch with the 4th Lincolns on their right, but could not get touch on the left, although some troops could be seen in the direction of S.12.c. At 4.55 p.m. 'A' Coy was ordered up as Reserve to 4th Lincolns and reached Railway cutting from S.11.c. central to S.11.a.2.8. getting in touch with 4th Lincolns there about 5.30 p.m. Till about 6.45 p.m. these Coys did considerable damage to the enemy while he was establishing M.G. posts on the RAVELSBERG Crest but later owing to the withdrawal of the troops on their left and the enemy's advance down the forward slopes from CRUCIFIX Corner, had to withdraw, 'C' Coy to the road from S.11.a.4.0 to S.11.a.9.4 and 'A' Coy to a line from S.11.c.5.7 to S.11.c.9.5 In this position these two Coys came under the orders of Major LAMBERTON (9th H.L.I.) and were disposed 'A' Coy in its original position and 'C' Coy on a line extending from A Coy's right flank about 400 yards almost S.W.

16th. About 12.30 am orders were received for the Battalion to withdraw through the 34th Division to SOUTHILL CAMP, where they arrived about 3.30 am with order to "Stand to" in the Camp at the usual hour. About 5.30 am orders were received for the Battalion to take up a position in artillery formation, in the area 'Close to the junction of, and between' the roads leading from BAILLEUL and DRANOUTRE to LOCRE. Arrived in position about 8.30 am. 4th & 5th Lincolns on left and 6/7 Royal Scots Fusiliers in front.
Orders to withdraw about 11.0 pm, and Battalion returned to SOUTHILL CAMP about 1.0 am 17th.

17th. Resumed position of support in road on slope on right of LOCRE-DRANOUTRE road about 9.0 am but were heavily shelled and forced to take up position in the open on the opposite side of valley near BAILLEUL-LOCRE Road, and dug accommodation for protection and concealment. Casualties about 80 including a few gas cases. Withdrew about 10.30 pm to CAMP on MONT ROUGE arriving about 12.30 am 18th.

18th. Resumed position in trenches dug on 17th. A Coy sent to 2nd Sherwoods and D Coy to 1st Leicesters both occupying parts of Red Line in Support.

E. Bigham Lt Col
Comdg 1/4 Leicester Regt

SECRET   ORIGINAL

Army Form C. 2118.

WAR DIARY
INTELLIGENCE SUMMARY.
(Erase heading not required.)

2/4 Lincolnshire Regt.

No 16

Place	Date	Hour	Summary of Events and Information	Remarks and references to Appendices
G.25.D.6.9	1/5/18		Quiet day. Battn digging SWITCH LINE and improving EAST POPERINGHE LINE. 6 pm to 11 pm Artillery active on KEMMEL FRONT.	AA.O
do	2/5/18		Quiet day. Trenches improved.	AA.O
do	3/5/18		Trenches improved.	AA.O
do	4/5/18		Work continued on WINDMILL DEFENCES. Very heavy artillery fire on KEMMEL front during afternoon & evening.	AA.O
do	5/5/18 2.30pm	Battn moved by march route to HOUTKERQUE arriving 6.30 pm. Battn H.Q. E.20.A.9.6. Sheet 27.	AA.O
Sheet 27 E.20.A.9.6	6/6/18 11 am	Battn moved by bus to NIEURLET. Battn H.Q. established at 3.D central at HAZEBROUCK, 5A.	AA.O
NIEURLET	7/5/18		Battn rested. G.O.C. presents medals for recent operations. Lt. Col. Sir John COLQUHOUN. Bart. D.S.O. received bar to D.S.O.	AA.O
do	8/5/18		3 officers & 76 O.R. proceeded to the base returning at ST OMER.	AA.O
do	9/6/18 6.30 am	Battn Training Cadre previous by march route to MANETZ arriving 2/5 p.m. Battn H.Q. S.D.9.6 (w) HAZEBROUCK 5A.	AA.O

"SECRET"

ORIGINAL

Army Form C. 2118.

WAR DIARY
or
INTELLIGENCE SUMMARY.

(Erase heading not required.)

2/4 LEICESTERSHIRE REGT

Instructions regarding War Diaries and Intelligence Summaries are contained in F. S. Regs., Part II. and the Staff Manual respectively. Title pages will be prepared in manuscript.

Place	Date	Hour	Summary of Events and Information	Remarks and references to Appendices
MAMETZ	10/5/18	10.30am	Battn Training Cadre moved by road route to PRESSY-LES-PERNES arriving 5.30pm. Battn H.Q. I.E. 6.7 (rof LENS 11)	HQQ
PRESSY-LES PERNES	11/5/18		Parties T.C. noted.	HQQ
do	12/5/18		CAPT JAMIE proceeded to Our H.Q. as Staff Learner. BDE H.Q. moved to ESTREE-CAUCHIE	HQQ
do	13/5/18		Warning order received for Battn Tr Cadre to move to ESTREE-CAUCHIE.	HQQ
do	14/5/18	10am	Battn Tr Cadre moved by Motor Lorry to ESTREE-CAUCHY. arriving	HQQ
		2pm	Battn H.Q. W.2.A central (rof Sheet 36.B) Battn Training Staff visited 15 GARRISON GUARD ESSEX REGT.	
ESTREE-CAUCHIE	15/5/18			HQQ
do	16/5/18		B.O. ADJUTANT & COY COMMANDERS reconnoitred B.B. line	HQQ
do	17/5/18		CAPT. OLIVER proceeded to 176 INF BDE to take over duties of Staff Captain	HQQ
do	18/5/18		Defence scheme prepared for B.B. line	HQQ

Col C.O.
H. Leyh.
O/C 2/4 Leicestershire Regt

ORIGINAL

Army Form C. 2118.

WAR DIARY
or
INTELLIGENCE SUMMARY. 2/4 LEICESTERSHIRE REGT.
(Erase heading not required.)

SECRET

Instructions regarding War Diaries and Intelligence Summaries are contained in F.S. Regs., Part II, and the Staff Manual respectively. Title pages will be prepared in manuscript.

Place	Date	Hour	Summary of Events and Information	Remarks and references to Appendices
ESTREE CAUCHIE	19/5/18	11.15a	Bde Church parade at H.Q. 23rd LIVERPOOL REGT. Bde Band in attendance. Both Tr Corps played. 2/5 LINCOLN T.C. at football lost 2-1	1.G.O
do	23/5/18		A/Capts MASTERS & GREAVES proceeded to 59 Div Lewis Gun School & C.R.E. "C" SECTOR respectively. Capt OLIVER returned from 178 Inf Bde.	2.G.O
do	26/5/18		Football Team proceeded to HOUDAIN. Played 4th LINCOLNS Lost 4-1.	3.G.O
do	29/5/18		Received warning orders to be in readiness to move to 16th Div	4.G.O
do	30/5/18		Warning order to move to 16 Div cancelled	5.G.O
do	31/5/18		Lt Col Un Jan Balguhoun took DSO assumed Command of Brigade. Capt B.B. Wynn took over duties of Staff Captain.	6.G.O

B F Capt
2/4 Leicestershire Regt

www.ingramcontent.com/pod-product-compliance
Lightning Source LLC
Chambersburg PA
CBHW081434160426
43193CB00013B/2279